LEVI  NOV 1 8 2004

W9-BJL-571

DISCARDED BY
MEMPHIS PUBLIC LIBRARY

window
basics
Easy & No-Sew Treatments

Better Homes and Gardens® Books
Des Moines, Iowa

Better Homes and Gardens® Books
An imprint of Meredith® Books

Window Basics
Editor: Linda Hallam
Design: The Design Office of Jerry J. Rank
Contributors: Susan Andrews, Tina Blanck, Brian Carter, Andrea Caughey, Judy Elkhoury,
    Nancy Ingram, Shannon Jernigan, Wade Scherrer, Donna Talley Wendt
Copy Chief: Terri Fredrickson
Managers, Book Production: Pam Kvitne, Marjorie J. Schenkelberg
Contributing Copy Editor: Lorraine Ferrell
Contributing Proofreaders: Becky Danley, Judy Friedman, Heidi Johnson
Indexer: Kathleen Poole
Electronic Production Coordinator: Paula Forest
Editorial and Design Assistants: Kaye Chabot, Mary Lee Gavin, Karen Schirm

Meredith® Books
Editor in Chief: James D. Blume
Design Director: Matt Strelecki
Managing Editor: Gregory H. Kayko
Executive Editor, Home Decorating and Design: Denise L. Caringer

Director, Sales, Special Markets: Rita McMullen
Director, Sales, Premiums: Michael A. Peterson
Director, Sales, Retail: Tom Wierzbicki
Director, Book Marketing: Brad Elmitt
Director, Operations: George A. Susral
Director, Production: Douglas M. Johnston

Better Homes and Gardens® **Magazine**
Editor in Chief: Karol DeWulf Nickell
Executive Interior Design Editor: Sandra S. Soria

Meredith Publishing Group
President, Publishing Group: Stephen M. Lacy

Meredith Corporation
Chairman and Chief Executive Officer: William T. Kerr
Chairman of the Executive Committee: E. T. Meredith III

Cover Photograph: Pieter Estersohn

Copyright © 2002 by Meredith Corporation, Des Moines, Iowa. First Edition.
All rights reserved. Printed in the United States of America.
Library of Congress Control Number: 2001135103
ISBN: 0-696-21321-4

All of us at Better Homes and Gardens® Books are dedicated to providing you with
information and ideas to enhance your home. We welcome your comments and suggestions.
Write to us at: Better Homes and Gardens Books, Home Decorating and Design Editorial
Department, 1716 Locust St., Des Moines, IA 50309-3023.

If you would like to purchase any of our home decorating and design, cooking, crafts,
gardening, or home improvement books, check wherever quality books are sold.
Or visit us at: bhgbooks.com

contents

getting started

If you have always wanted to try your hand at creating your own window treatments, now is the perfect time. Decorating trends of paring down and lightening up mean that interior designers are leading the way to simple, softly constructed window treatments. Instead of the opulence of lined, interlined, and elaborately trimmed draperies with swags and jabots, designers are choosing tailored styles such as fabric panels hung from exposed hardware with minimal or no top treatments. Likewise, sheers, which let in light and views, are increasingly popular for window treatments and for chic portieres, draperies used as room dividers.

If you have basic sewing skills or would like to try no-sew home decor projects, window treatments are a natural starting point. Easy-sew or ready-made drapery panels, window scarves, or curtains can be embellished with trims and hung from interesting hardware for fashionable looks. Before you start your project, consider your needs for privacy and sun control. This determines whether you need operable treatments, which can be opened or closed, and whether lined or unlined panels or shades best suit your windows. Next, take into account how rooms relate to each other throughout your home. Use Home Tour, Chapter One, as a guide to creating a harmonious whole-house plan. Plan styles, colors, and fabrics before you begin to ensure continuity between rooms. Then work room by room as your time and budget allow. **Designers often use similar treatments in rooms that open to each other** or share the same style of furnishings, such as living and dining rooms. If window styles and sizes vary in a room, the same fabric is often used but in different fabrications, such as Roman shades and drapery panels. As you design your treatments, **keep**

in mind the mood of your decorating and existing furnishings and fabrics. For the most pleasing look, match the degree of formality of fabrics and styles in your window treatments to your room settings. You will see in Chapters Two through Four how window treatments **enhance every room of the house,** including kitchens, children's rooms, and nurseries.

Well-designed window treatments **provide the finishing touches for polished settings.** Basic styles such as drapery panels or shades work in a variety of settings from contemporary to country, depending on fabrics, trims, and applied detailing. In this book, you may find fabric choices in one featured style, and find the trim, detailing, or hardware you like in another example. **Mix and match ideas to create a personal look** that works for you. To translate your ideas into window treatments, **turn to Chapter Five for specific directions,** including time and skill estimates as well as materials lists for featured projects.

hometour

Enhance Classic Windows

Plan tailored styles and airy treatments that translate into a whole-house design scheme.

TAKE ADVANTAGE OF INTERESTING WINDOW STYLES AND DETAILING WITH TREATMENTS THAT HIGHLIGHT RATHER THAN HIDE. Focus on two or three classic styles, such as drapery panels and tailored Roman shades. In rooms where privacy or light or temperature control aren't major concerns, keep your look simply chic with breezy unlined panels, stylish sheers, or valances. If you are unsure of how much coverage you want, start with a valance. Then add side panels, blinds, or shades later if you find you need to control the exposure. For interest, vary fabrics, detailing, and trims. If you have recently moved into a new house or apartment or begun a whole-house redecorating project, plan window treatments that enhance the shapes and trims of your windows. Take your time and shop fabric outlets and fabric store sales or survey what is available ready-made to stretch your decorating budget. If you like vintage looks, shop flea markets or thrift stores for old linens or interesting items that can be repurposed as drapery rods, finials, or tiebacks.

■ A patterned cafe sheer lightly dresses the large arched window in the living room of a 1920s California Spanish Colonial Revival house, *left*. Because the arched window is a hallmark of this classic style and the focal point of the room, only the lower half is covered to provide a degree of privacy and to diffuse light. The decorative black iron hardware recalls hardware often used in houses of the period. The sheer repeats as drapery panels for the casement window—illustrating the lesson of using the same fabric in different treatment styles chosen for compatibility with window shapes. The swagged valance with fringed trim and the wrought-iron hardware finish the handsome treatment. The valance serves as visual balance to the beams and high ceiling, creating a pleasing counterpoint to the arched window.

See pages 85 and 86 for how-to directions.

■ Pulled to the side with a tieback, one drapery panel dresses each dining room window, *below left*. Rings, sewn on each panel, hang from the wrought-iron rods with attention-getting, spear-like finials. The beauty of this simple treatment is in the floral damask fabric, cut deliberately long enough to pool on the floor, and in the embellishment of an antique red fringe. The panels are lined with ivory sateen to extend the life of the damask. However, unlined drapery panels accomplish a similar look with minimal sewing. Such a simple, yet sophisticated treatment, which requires minimal fabric, is ideal for rooms with narrow windows or little natural light. Drapery panels without heavy top treatments illustrate the trend toward lighter, pared-down traditional decorating. **See page 87 for how-to directions.**

■ A combination of Roman shades, each detailed with an inverted, crescent-shaped valance, and fixed sheers provide privacy in the master bedroom, *below center*. Because the French doors face a busy street, the sheer panels are

attached with rods at the top and bottom. Roman shades guarantee additional privacy as needed, but can be raised for light. Lined Roman shades are an ideal treatment for rooms such as bedrooms that require varying degrees of privacy. Extra black-out lining can be added to block out street lights or daylight. Because Roman shades are a tailored fabrication, they translate into contemporary as well as traditional settings. **See page 88 for how-to directions.**

▌ Window treatments work with paint as economical decorating tools to update older bath tiles and fixtures. In the pink and black master bath, *below right,* the Roman shades refresh the decor with lively stripes while adding a practical covering. The Art Deco ambience of the bath inspires the fanciful bottom trim. Black and silver braid, enhanced with two-toned lavender beaded fringe, recalls the glamorous 1920s. An interesting trim is an easy, add-on touch to personalize the tailored look of the classic shades. **See pages 82–84 for Roman shade directions.**

▌ Fabricated into a Roman shade, a lively print in kaleidoscopic colors covers the powder room's sole window, *above left.* The pennant-style valance, trimmed with yellow braid, details the simple style. While such an energetic print might overpower a larger room if used on multiple windows, the fabric adds interest to the small powder room. The yellow wall color picks up a shade in the multihued fabric. **See pages 82–84 for Roman shade directions.**

▌ Long Roman shades cover French windows to a balcony, yet can be raised for light and views, *above center.* The print fabric repeats in the comforter and table skirt, a pleasing way to create harmony in a small bedroom. A length of ball fringe, attached at the ends of the headers, swags in a crescent shape at the top of the shades. The simple accent contributes a touch of whimsy to the treatment. **See page 89 for how-to directions.**

▌ Depending on window style and location, the simplest window treatment may be more effective and stylish than an overly elaborate or formal one. In this kitchen breakfast nook, *right,* a lighthearted fruit print is fabricated into a shapely valance that defines the window without blocking light. For a shirred effect, the valance features a rod pocket top. For extra body and a finished look, a small border of coordinating print trims the lower edge. While this valance is shaped and lined, an unlined, tightly woven fabric, cut and hemmed from a length of fabric, is an easy substitute. The black iron rod repeats the style of the light fixture. **See page 89 for how-to directions.**

Lightly Defined Accents

Welcome the sunshine with airy sheers and lush but unlined window treatments that diffuse without blocking light and views.

AS WINDOW TREATMENTS SIMPLIFY AND EVEN TOP TREATMENTS PARE DOWN, FABRICS, FABRICATION, AND TRIM DETERMINE THE FORMALITY. If you want to emulate this look, consider what part window treatments will play in your overall and room-by-room decorating scheme. Minimize dramatic patterns and bright or deep colors, and decorate with sheers, pale tones, and vintage fabrics and fragments. When your window-treatment style is minimal but you need privacy and sun control, include operable white or off-white shades or blinds. As an easy alternative, look for ready-made panels to hang from vintage or reproduction hardware. To get the most from the panels, adapt them to your personal style by sewing metal drapery rings or ribbons as needed to attach to rods.

■ Ready-made tab-top drapery panels hang from metal leaf-motif wall hangings found at a flea market, *left*. Although the wall hangings were designed to hang vertically, they work equally well hung horizontally. Distressed corbels, salvaged architectural fragments, find new life as alternatives to more conventional tiebacks. In a setting without a window seat, wall-mounted tiebacks or conventional fabric ties would substitute.

■ Originally associated with country-style curtains, ready-made tab-top panels, *right*, lend themselves to a variety of decorating styles. The lushness of the cut velvet sheers adapts well to a coolly serene living room.

■ Two shades of unlined silk create a simple yet sumptuous window treatment for a casually elegant dining room, *opposite*. In a scheme based on minimal color, the fabrics contrast for a distinctive color block effect. The division of the panel into two-thirds taupe and one-third peach bands is more visually pleasing than bands of even lengths, and reinforces the classic design rule of thirds. For a neat appearance, the panels are simply sewn with a rod pocket header and shirred on a painted rod, hung at window height. Decorative finials adorn the ends of the rod. Fabric pools slightly on the polished oak floor. **See page 90 for how-to directions.**

■ A loosely woven natural fabric echoes the country cottage style of the two pairs of painted chairs, *above*. The valances are sewn with rod pocket headers for easy attachment. Bits of vintage trim and buttons are hand-sewn to the hems. The height of a window determines valance proportions, with the treatment usually covering most or all of the top pane. **See page 90 for how-to directions.**

■ A basic tension rod, *right,* is the only hardware necessary to convert a 1940s dresser scarf into a charming kitchen window treatment. Decorative linens from the 1930s and the 1940s are good candidates for such easy window treatments. While older linens may be too fragile or too worn, hand-embroidered and trimmed linens of that era can be found in good condition or require only touch-up mending. If a linen has yellow spots, launder with a nonabrasive, phosphate-free soap; do not use chlorine bleach. Or try the natural method of carefully rubbing lemon juice and salt over stains and hanging the piece to dry in the sun.

■ A piece with crochet in pristine condition is a find for a window treatment, *below.* If the crochet is soiled, presoak the piece for 15 minutes in clear water before laundering. Rinse and press while slightly damp before hanging.

■ Matching pairs of table squares, *opposite,* are often the perfect size and shape for converting into lighthearted kitchen or breakfast nook window treatments. Here the squares are folded into pennants; three vintage buttons are stitched in place to create pockets for the basic tension rods. Collected linens look best when washed, lightly starched, and ironed before being reused as window treatments.

The delicate trim of linens from the 1930s and the 1940s contributes to their renewed appeal as simply chic window treatments, *left*. Oversize vintage buttons are a find that complete the look. If it is difficult to locate matched buttons, mismatched ones can be equally charming. If older table squares are unavailable, oversize European or American souvenir tea towels can be cut or folded for novel stand-ins.

Light and Privacy

Address the typical concerns of city living with treatments that seclude without blocking air or sun.

OLDER RESIDENCES OFFER DESIGN CHALLENGES AS WELL AS CHARM, ESPECIALLY WHEN IT COMES TO WINDOWS. If you live in an urban area or on a busy street, operable treatments that close completely at night and muffle sound can be a necessity. When windows are small or used for seasonal cooling, treatments need to softly diffuse without darkening the room or stifling the breeze. Operable drapery panels and various fabrications of sheers offer practical solutions.

The best window treatments enhance a room's decorating scheme and, when necessary, solve a design challenge. The drapery panel, *below*, amplifies the Asian ambience of a serene reading nook with the kimono-style panels, sewn as color blocks of fabrics. The purchased sheer center panel lets in light and air while blocking the view of a nearby house. **See page 92 for how-to directions.**

Traditional drapery panels, in dark taupe and cream fabrics, puddle luxuriously in the bay window. The tiebacks allow the panels to close at night for privacy as well as provide a degree of warmth in winter. While the panels are a classic way to dress a bay window, the choice of fabrics, sewn as color blocks, and the contemporary iron rings and rod update the look. Neutral, subdued fabrics create a versatile backdrop and allow collections and furnishings to star in the sophisticated scheme. **See page 91 for how-to directions.**

The two treatment styles in this dining room, *right,* illustrate the versatility of fashionable sheer fabric. Panels sewn with rod pocket headers hang gracefully to the floor over a double-hung window. Softly tailored Roman shades cover higher casement windows, open in the summer for ventilation. While sheers are associated with breezy panels or swagged drapery scarves, tailored fabrication into shades is a fresh, innovative look. Dining chairs are slipcovered in matching sheer fabric to unify the scheme. **See pages 93 and 94 for how-to directions.**

A trio of ready-made drapery panels from a discount store, detailed with blue banding, *below,* provides a custom look at a fraction of the time and expense. For interest, side panels hang over the banded center panel gathered with a tieback. As a no-sew alternative, pair colored side panels with a sheer or white center panel and use wide ribbon or thick cording for tiebacks. To create a romantic look, choose ecru or white lace panels and tie with lace or satin ribbon. **See page 92 for how-to directions.**

A covered header strip and simple sewing transform a vintage tablecloth with crochet inserts into a softly gathered shade, *above.* Linens, finds at tag sales and flea markets, evoke a cottage or country look that is appropriate to the stained or painted trim and woodwork of older houses—or to country-style kitchens in newer houses. Here the ecru fabric and crochet soften and lighten the oak trim. As an alternative, a soft cotton fabric, such as muslin, can be gathered in the same style and trimmed with new or vintage crochet.

Sized to fit the panes, the striped panel, *below left,* allows a casement window to open for ventilation with a degree of privacy. The blue stripes, rather than standard white, enliven a hall window. The rod pocket ensures a neat finish while the beaded trim details with a lighthearted touch. Accents, such as the trim, elevate standard treatments into stylish design statements. **See page 93 for how-to directions.**

Glass drawer knobs and applied beaded trim update a purchased sheer panel into a glamorous window treatment, *below right.* Pre-drilled holes make it easy to screw the knobs into the window trim. Comparable variations and embellishments turn inexpensive, standard panels from discount and home furnishings stores and decorating catalogs into one-of-a-kind treatments. While this delicate trim is hand-sewn, hot gluing is another option. **See page 94 for how-to directions.**

living&dining

Welcome natural light into your living and dining rooms with pared-down panels and glamorous prints that meld the best of traditional and contemporary styles.

living&dining

SIMPLE SOPHISTICATION. Lighten and brighten your living and dining rooms with side panels that frame and define. As part of the design trend toward edited interiors, window treatments even for formal rooms are sleek and simple with or without top treatments. If you want treatments to admit as much light as possible, opt for unlined panels that softly diffuse. To achieve a more structured shape and to protect fabric from sun bleaching, line the panels or protect unlined panels with shades or blinds.

Purchased drapery scarves, cut in half, serve as panels in a refined living room, *right*. Drapery rods hang below the crown molding to elevate the ceiling visually. The straight lines of the panels contrast with the curves of the armchairs, coffee table, and mirrored sconce for the energy of contrasting shapes. **See page 96 for how-to directions.**

In a living room with the ambience of an English country house, faux leopard fabric relaxes traditional furniture, notably the tufted leather Chesterfield sofa, *opposite*. Sewn to iron rings, the banded panels hang from a twisted iron rod with palm-tree-motif finials. The fabric and exposed hardware reinforce the around-the-world feel of the sculpture, Oriental rug, and traditional and contemporary art. **See page 95 for how-to directions.**

HEAD START WITH READY-MADES. Browse catalogs or home decor stores for inspiration for your own one-of-a-kind window treatments. Simple embellishments such as hardware, hand-sewn trim, or painted details elevate basic treatments into design statements. Plan your treatments as part of a coordinated decorating and color scheme for a polished, pulled-together look.

Ready-made sailcloth drapery panels and natural cotton Roman shades, *right,* initiate practical starting points to a lively, lighthearted window treatment. Handpainting and sponging with fabric paint personalize the canvas shades and the coordinating banding, sewn to the purchased panels. The curves of the sponged tulips and hand-painted vines echo the decorative pulls of the vintage chest. The repetition of the upbeat red hue unifies the young and happy decorating scheme. The contrast of red and green, opposites on the color wheel, energizes the living area. **See page 97 for how-to directions.**

Light sponging imparts a painterly feel to the stylized tulips, *above left.* Diamonds are hand-painted, following marked guidelines for neatness. Circles are also sponged. As alternatives, commercial stencils or stamps could be used in place of sponges, or if a looser effect is desired, all the painting could be freehand. The swing drapery rods, with extensions, allow the panels to frame the detailed shades. Cording neatly joins the seamed panels for a professional appearance.

GARDEN-STYLE DECORATING.

Invite the outdoors inside with window treatments that incorporate natural elements and motifs. If you enjoy decorating in the popular garden or country looks, opt for simple window treatments with the same feel as your own well-loved and gently aged pieces. Personal touches, rather than opulent fabrics or elaborate fabrications, are paramount in this simple, from-the-heart style. For an updated version of country cottage, select edited looks that replace ruffles and bows with fabric panels or sheers.

The relaxed spirit of this sitting room, *left,* calls for an equally easygoing window treatment. In harmony with the distressed finishes of the iron daybed and wood table, natural raffia ties a sheer fabric panel to a gently curved tree branch. The woven storage cubes repeat the natural elements of branch and raffia. **See page 95 for how-to directions.**

Iron bird finials, tapped into predrilled holes, appear to perch on the tree-branch drapery rod, *above right.* Depending on the design direction, other motifs for finials, such as the widely used French fleur-de-lis, would be stylish finishing touches. For a fuller look, two fabric panels could be tied to the tree branch. Or if framing the window is the goal, panels could be tied from a longer branch that extends beyond the window width. Fabric and ties should be lightweight to avoid weighing down a branch.

DOUBLE THE IMPACT. Use the anchor of a pair of chairs and a classic window treatment to create a strong design statement. Arrange the chairs at the window, and design a symmetrical window treatment. The idea works well for a range of decorating styles, creating a sense of order from the obviously symmetrical arrangement. The key: Choose a treatment style and fabric compatible with your chairs.

Tailored drapery panels, sewn from two fabrics and a deep fringe trim, appear as a clean, more contemporary backdrop for a pair of armless upholstered chairs, *above.* Black repeats in the fabrics and trim to unify the scheme. The classic iron drapery rod barely tops the window casing. **See page 96 for how-to directions.**

Black and white against the yellow wall, *right,* further animates the lively scheme. The banded fringe grazes the floor without puddling. As an alternative, the houndstooth panels can be lengthened to the floor or allowed to puddle.

Mid-20th-century design joins popular decorating directions as part of the trend to edited interiors. Here, grouped with a pair of sleek 20th-century chairs, is another staple of the era: Roll-up bamboo shades, *below*, accent with casual tropical flair. The treatment creates a subtle and pleasing backdrop for the shapely mid-century furniture. The squared-off lines of the cornices, actually folded and stapled from ordinary kraft paper, repeat the boxy shapes of the tufted chair backs. The small woven table, in a pleasing round configuration, reinforces the texture of the bamboo. Available from import stores and decorating catalogs, bamboo shades are easy to install and operable when sun control or privacy is important. **See page 98 for how-to directions.**

A standard 1×2 board, cut to the window width, hides support for the stapled kraft paper cornice, *right*. The light brown color of the basic kraft paper, from an art supply store, blends easily with the color striations of the bamboo slats.

SPELL IT OUT. Consider the space between your window treatment and the ceiling molding as a decorating opportunity to tap. While it often works well to hang window treatments directly under the molding, the wall lends itself to other options for detailing and display. For the freshest looks, gravitate to simple, personal ideas.

The banded sheer panels, *right,* serve as the supporting player to the attention-getting brass letters, tapped into predrilled holes above. The letters, which spell out "good friend" in French, set the tone for a comfortable sitting area in a family living room. As an economical and easy substitute for a hardware application, the sheer panel hangs, via basic buttonholes, from brass hand-hewn nails. While the sheers add softness and touches of blue, standard blinds are used to guarantee privacy and sun control. As a finishing touch, the stems of vintage metal flowers from a flea market work as decorative tiebacks. **See page 98 for how-to directions.**

Reminiscent of fabric from the 1920s and 1930s, the crisp stripes are sewn vertically and horizontally for the unlined, banded treatment, *left.* The buttonholes are machine-made, but could be cut and hand-sewn. Possibilities with brass letters are endless—from a child's name to "welcome" or "good luck" in English or another language.

Simple tab-top ties in a natural fabric replace drapery rings for a valance fabricated from an Asian-inspired pictorial print, *left*. The two-inch burlap banding adds a neatly finished look as the fabric repeats the ties. The casual Roman shade, created from burlap, complements the valance. Matching eyelash fringe adorns the shade. **See page 100 for how-to directions.**

A bamboo cane from a garden shop, *below,* takes on a new role as a stylish curtain rod. Canes can be cut easily to fit the window width. For wider openings, such as porches, multiple canes are connected by slipping them over a dowel. Fabric strips are knotted, rather than tied into bows, for a casual effect appropriate to the fabric and room setting.

TIED-ON DETAILING. Use tied-on panels and valances as an easy, budget-stretching alternative to treatments decorated with trims and elaborate fabrications. Depending on the fabric and length, tied-on treatments can be as casual or as formal as you wish. For a quick treatment, sew ribbon strips to ready-made panels or valances.

With simple treatments, fabric choice sets the formality. In this elegant dining room, *opposite,* shantung silk dupioni panels grace a dining room entry and frame the courtyard view. The iron drapery rod, from a mail-order catalog, features moon-like spheres as finials. **See page 99 for how-to directions.**

REFINED TREATMENTS. When you want to create a dressy or dramatic living or dining room, call upon the style-setting power of window treatments. When fabric is your choice, keep this designer adage in mind: Generous yardage of an inexpensive fabric is a richer look than skimpy yardage of an expensive fabric. If you do fall in love with an expensive fabric, use it as a luxurious top treatment over lavish panels of a more economically priced fabric.

■ Abundant yardage, seven yards per panel, imparts the elegance of a glamourous ball gown, *below*. Panels hang from an iron rod, flush to the wall for a contemporary touch.

A no-sew treatment seldom looks more stylish than the bouffant style that defines this living room, *above.* Designed by a decorator who enjoys the fun of no-sew effects, the elaborate color-coordinated swags and panels are created from two fabrics—a plaid and a botanical print. While one fabric can be used alone or as the double-swag style shown here, the contrast of the featured fabrics contributes to the appeal of the total treatment. Fastened to long roofing nails with rubber bands, the treatment is actually easier to create than it looks. While the polished cotton fabric chosen for this room has excellent body, which allows it to maintain shape once styled, tissue paper or bridal netting can be used as stuffing to pouf swags. **See page 101 for how-to directions.**

Salvaged vintage shutters, *left,* frame the vista from the dining room into the garden. The operable shutters are hinged and then attached to the door frame to close for sun control or for privacy at night.

SHEER BEAUTIES. When you want to diffuse light or mask a less-than-beautiful window or view, consider the decorative assets of stylish sheers. Because sheers are available in an array of colors and designs, they lend themselves to the stylish edited traditional and softened contemporary looks.

▊ Furnished with an eclectic mix of traditional and country pieces, the dining room, *left,* takes on a lighter, less serious tone with loosely hung sheers at the windows. The casualness of the sheers contrasts with the embellished mantel, antique chairs, and colorful rug. The subtle treatment allows the furniture arrangement to star in the scheme.

▊ Sheer fabrics are ideal for portieres, *opposite,* which are draperies used for separation or privacy. Here, in a contemporary living space, a pair of portieres, sewn from an orange sheer fabric, divide and define without blocking light. In a white-and-neutral scheme, the orange energizes with an unexpected, welcome jolt of color. In this tailored application, the banded panels hang via small drapery rings from ceiling-mounted rods. Small rings enhance a neatly tailored style as the panels hangclose to the rods. The rings also allow panels to slide easily.

bed&bath

bed&bath

Design treatments that contribute style and fun as they solve your needs for privacy.

ROMANS ALWAYS WORK. Consider your specific needs for privacy, light control, and insulation. Roman shades, a versatile decorating staple, are likely to solve these needs. If you prefer darkness for sleeping, sew lined Roman shades in a weighty fabric. The window-fitting design and the folds effectively shut out light when the shades are down. The same feature makes Roman shades excellent insulators and noise mufflers as well. You may want to mount the shade inside or outside the window frame. Outside mounts offer the best results for insulation and blocking light, but inside mounts show off more window frame.

A trio of Roman shades, *right,* enhances the colorful background of a youthful bedroom, anchored by an old-fashioned, early-20th-century iron bed. The tailored style of the shade, strengthened by the fabric choice and the precise banding, provides a more contemporary counterpoint to the country style of the bed and linens. The colorful cotton fabric chosen for the shades plays off the red and white checks of the dust ruffle and decorative pillows while energetically contrasting with the green walls. The shades are mounted inside the frame to show off the architectural detail of the painted-wood trim. **See page 102 for how-to directions.**

NURSERY NAPPING. When your goal is to encourage daytime napping—and later morning wake-up—Roman shades that block are ideal. A whimsical print enlivens the scheme of a nursery or child's room. Avoid frequent redecorating by selecting fabric that your baby will not soon outgrow.

SAFETY ALERT: Purchase the new cordless blinds or shades, or check that all cords and strings are out of your baby's reach. Children have been strangled on blind cords that do not meet safety standards. Wrap cords around wall-mounted cleats, and pull the bed away from the window. Cut cord loops, and cover cut ends with end caps available at fabric stores.

Because blocking the light is paramount, shades are mounted outside the window frame in this nursery, *left.* The room, painted a restful blue, is simply furnished with white furniture. The stylized print, based on mid-20th-century children's designs, sets the playful tone every nursery needs. **See pages 104–105 for how-to directions.**

Ball fringe, *below,* adds the detail that elevates a cotton-print shade to a charming accent. Trim can be topstitched or hot glued to the shade.

HIGH-STYLE HARDWARE. If your bedroom is small or without architectural detailing, design window treatments that mirror the casual chic of 21st-century decorating. Hang your easy or no-sew treatments high as a soft, graceful backdrop to your bed and other furnishings. Because such treatments are normally unlined for gentle draping, shades or blinds are often added when privacy or light control is needed.

Unlined, simple-sew panels of print fabric hang from flea market iron hangers installed at ceiling height, *below.* The print creates a private-bower feel in the small room. **See page 99 for how-to directions.**

Gently flowing, ready-made drapery panels hang from repurposed drawer pulls, *above,* in a tiny bedroom where inches count. The secret to the look: Every other tie is removed from the ready-made sheer panels for a softer, looser drape behind the bed. Two of the extra ties are hand-sewn inside the panels for tiebacks that flank the pair of windows. The simplicity of the softly tailored treatment works with the eclectic furnishings and maintains a youthful scheme. In chilly climates, the summery sheers can be replaced with heavier lined panels detailed in the same way for winter months.

Predrilled holes allow standard ivory-colored drawer pulls, *left,* to screw into the wall below the crown molding. Glass or hand-painted pulls offer other options. The pale shades of the pulls and sheer repeat the light trim and offer striking contrast against the wall hue.

BATH BEAUTIES. Have fun with your bathroom window treatments. As these spaces are typically the smallest rooms in a residence, sometimes with only one window, the window treatment can be the style setter in the confined space.

▌ Banded fabric panels transform the bath in an older cottage-style home into a luxurious retreat, *below.* Such treatments, fabricated from washable fabric, are ideal for baths with less-than-perfect walls.

An old-fashioned faucet and enamel sink handles, *left,* echo the hardware of the vintage sink and the clawfoot tub shown on page 54. The clever repurposing illustrates the decorating power of whimsical touches. The gently swagged, unlined valance softens the look while the panel, held securely in place with a pair of tension rods, ensures privacy. Attached with hook-and-loop tape, the gathered sink skirt enhances the cottage style.

No-sew treatments, such as the painted shade and tied canvas valance, *below,* provide flair in a family bathroom. For a bathroom without a view, an artist lightly sketched then painted the stylized urn in front of an arched window, an easy interpretation of trompe l'oeil, French for "fool the eye." The tied valance is stapled and folded. Hand-painted dots detail the ties, cut from duck cloth. **See page 103 for how-to directions.**

All is calm in the nursery, *left,* where draperies fabricated from vintage white-on-white chenille and antique matelassé bedspreads hang artfully from a birch tree trunk used as the drapery pole. A French child's hat, in the style of a jester's cap with knotted ends, inspires the zigzag valance. Angle irons, painted to match the wall, hold the birch log securely in place at ceiling height.

Grapevines adorn the tops of the window treatment, *below,* for a natural finishing touch. To avoid breaking the vines, the treatment designer uses fresh stems and wets them for pliability. Here, the vines are twisted up and over the decorative birch pole.

Theatrical gauze, *opposite,* from a theatrical supply store pairs with birch log poles for a sophisticated master bedroom treatment. Gauze is an economical and dramatic alternative to more expensive fabrics. The material works well alone or lightly lined for a translucent look that filters light while maintaining privacy. Here the tops are shirred and tied with roping to the birch pole. Roman shades match the neutral wall color.

NATURAL STYLE. The decorating trend to natural materials from the garden and forest offers possibilities for window treatments that echo a growing interest in the environment. If one of your goals is to create serene, soothing bedrooms for you and your children, consider the benefits of recycling logs, vines, and branches and repurposing vintage fabrics. Work with natural colors, shades of white, and wood tones. Introduce textures, such as wicker and rattan, for furnishings that reflect the style.

COTTAGE GARDEN. Put pretty finishing touches on a girl's room or nursery with window treatments that animate the happy setting. To stretch your decorating budget, work with styles that showcase lighthearted detailing without calling for quantities of fabrics and trims. If you must use blinds or fabric shades for light control, keep cords safely out of the reach of children or buy the newer cordless shades or blinds to prevent accidental strangling.

Covered buttons artfully trim the decorative valance in a garden-fresh girl's room, *above,* where the hand-painted wall flowers star. The youthful print repeats for the sham ruffle and bed skirt, an ideal way to unify simple details into a decorating scheme. Ready-made sheers are a stylish budget stretcher. **See page 106 for how-to directions.**

The easy-tie stagecoach valance treatments, *below,* introduce cheery pattern and color while minimizing sewing time and fabric yardage. The lively print also inspires the decorating scheme from the sunny wall color to the artfully painted and detailed rocking chair and painted floorcloth. The print covers the piped window seat and reappears as a pillow and cushion on the hand-painted rocking chair. Because the print is a geometric without figurative motif, the treatments will work well as the baby grows up or if the room is later used for guests. **See page 103 for how-to directions.**

YOUNG AND FUN. Impart lighthearted style to a child's room with a window treatment that is part of the scene. As you start the decorating project, let your child in on the fun, and work together on the theme and color scheme. Take your child along as you shop for fabrics and furnishings. It is often easier to choose the window treatment as a first step, and then pull out a blending or complementary wall color.

▋ In this girl's room, planned to grow up gracefully, the fashionable window treatment, *opposite,* accents a pair of French doors, dressed with louvered shutters for privacy. The poufed panels, fabricated from the toile-like print, set the fresh green and print scheme that updates the antique bed and rocker. Panels are lined for body, and pulled through scarf rings mounted above the door frame. Crumpled tissue paper gives the poufs the desired fullness. **See page 104 for how-to directions.**

▋ The pennant-style treatment, *above left,* conjures fairy tales of knights, jesters, and jousting in a boy's room with an updated medieval theme. The color block fabric, trimmed in black banding, suggests the stained glass of castles and cathedrals, and stands out against the rich red walls. A jester-hat pillow repeats the red and blue colors. **See page 108 for how-to directions.**

▋ Window treatments, such as this pair based on pennants, *above right,* denote a decorating theme without elaborate wallpapers or hand-painted murals. These treatments use minimal fabric and are attached with hook-and-loop tape to conceal mounting boards. Accessories echo the idea of the current medieval theme. Walls are dramatically but simply treated with red paint. Because these treatments are tailored and the walls are painted, the room will adapt easily to its young resident's changing tastes. Sports memorabilia is an easy switch.

See page 108 for how-to directions.

Ready-made sheer panels hung from swing-arm extension rods, *left,* create a sense of privacy and enclosure in a bedroom. Panels are hand-stitched to rings, rather than shirred on a rod pocket, for loose drapes. The swing-arm rods move easily to control the light during the day. For detailing, the stylized vine motifs hand-painted on the wall also can be hand-painted on the sheers with fabric paint. As an alternative, lace panels can be tied to the rods with green or yellow ribbons.

Inspired by the butterfly gardens of summer, this no-sew treatment, *opposite,* infuses a young girl's bedroom with the charms of a walk in the country. Fabric-store nylon netting in a 54-inch width wraps around a painted rod and hangs gracefully to the floor. For detailing, butterflies from a crafts supply store are spaced casually over the treatment as though they have just landed. Thin wire from a crafts supply store holds them securely in place. As an alternative, stylized insects or flowers can be wired to the netting. Here oversize flowers and grass blades are hand-painted on the wall to achieve the day-in-the-garden decorating theme. A trimmed straw hat finishes the setting in old-fashioned style.

SHEER DELIGHTS. Gently define spaces and add softness with light-diffusing sheers and nylon netting. These gentle treatments elicit images of open windows and summer breezes, pleasant complements to country, cottage, and garden decorating styles. To save time, look for ready-made sheer panels that can be updated with style-setting hardware. In addition to white and off-white sheers, consider the decorating impact of pale pastels or subtle woven patterns.

MAPS OF THE WORLD. Explore the world with window treatments showcasing the decorative and educational assets of standard maps. Because maps are fascinating to students and collectors alike, it is easy to find new maps with the most accurate and current names for countries, as well as reproductions of older maps. Consider current world or country maps as a learning tool in a child's bedroom or playroom. If you or someone in your family is a history buff, base a treatment on a map of particular interest, such as the Roman Empire or pre-World War I or World War II Europe.

Animate a bedroom, home office, den, or playroom with color-coded maps of Europe as shown here, *opposite,* or another continent or hemisphere of the world. The project is easy because the technique is based on the fusible shade kits sold at fabric stores. In this project, standard paper maps replace fabric for lively pull-down shades. Because the fun of the project comes from the map motifs, choose furnishings and decorations that make educational window treatments the stars of the room. To enhance the theme, frame posters highlighting regional cities, or add road-map pillows to a sofa or chair.
See page 107 for how-to directions.

For doubled interest, a map-motif valance, cut to the shapes of the continents, pairs with an embellished standard pull-down shade, *right.* The valance hangs on rings from a decorative brass rod finished with painted sphere finials. Roping finishes in nautical style.
See page 107 for how-to directions.

kitchens, etc.

kitchens, etc.

Enjoy your casual living spaces with lighthearted and easy window treatments.

MODERN COUNTRY. Take advantage of the relaxed attitude of your kitchen and other informal family gathering spots. Choose easy-care treatments that welcome the light for these naturally casual rooms. It's a good idea to choose washable treatments or simply constructed treatments that can be dry-cleaned. While the design trend is toward light, airy, and unconstructed styles, add bifold shutters, blinds, or shades when privacy or sun control is a concern. Because messy cords can be a problem at sink windows, consider cordless shades and blinds, available through home decor stores and home centers.

▌ The simple tea towel window treatment, *right,* imparts a cottage touch to a sleek kitchen with overtones of country. The white fabric, with woven red accents, repeats the white molding above the stove and the white dinnerware. No hardware is needed for installation. Instead, three grommets punched along one side allow the treatment to hang from old-fashioned cup hooks screwed into the window frame. A clothespin pinches and shapes the towel on each side. A matching tea towel hangs from a nearby hook. The pattern of tea towels, from European Country to vintage American towels, sets the look of the easy treatment.

ART OF THE SHADE. Dress up a white or plain kitchen with a style-setting window treatment. For the most current look, choose a fabric that appeals to you, and then let it star in the window treatments. Interesting patterns and motifs, rather than elaborate fabrications, work best in the kitchen.

▍Detailed enough to stand in for art, this rooster novelty print fabric, banded in a subtle stripe, translates into tailored Roman shades, o*pposite*. Novelty prints refer to accurately detailed motifs copied on fabrics. Other typical motifs often used for kitchens include tea cups, fruits, vegetables, animals, and gardening tools. **See page 109 for how-to directions.**

▍A tailored Roman shade without a header provides the ideal fabrication for a novelty print because the pattern is clearly visible whether the shade is lowered partially or completely. The breakfast room repeats the kitchen treatment to tie the spaces together, *above*. The painted rooster gracing the table continues the lighthearted look. Iron shelves and photographs echo the black fabric background for a definite note of sophisticated style.

▍Striped banding matches a shade of yellow gold from the rooster print as it contrasts with the black and earthy red shades, *left*. In rooms where window treatments serve as art, such banding reinforces the appeal. As an alternative, a shade can be fabricated without banding and trimmed along the lower edge.

Softly gathered on old dinner forks bent into curtain rings, a cotton leaf-motif print valance tops a sink window, *below.* Here the leaf motif reaffirms the soothing mood of the soft green-and-white scheme. The simple valance maximizes the impact of a tiny bit of fabric, an ideal way to take advantage of a fabric remnant or a bit of a vintage linen. The fabric width is only slightly wider than the window for the gentle drape between rings. A tailored treatment measures the width of the window plus the seam allowances for hems. For a fuller look, the width of the window is doubled for the valance. A row of trim can be hand-sewn or hot glued as the edging.

FABRIC ACCENTS. When you want your kitchen windows to welcome the sun, think of treatments that accent and define without blocking light or view. Look for interesting new or vintage fabric—you won't need much for these simple styles—and for hardware that is part of the look. Little or minimal sewing is all that is required to dress a kitchen window in style.

Corners of a 1940s tablecloth introduce a breezy touch to a Southwest-style kitchen, *above.* The pair of decorative telescope rods screw into the window frame, one on each side, contributing interest and detail to the easy treatment. The stylized 1940s and 1950s fruit and vegetable motifs in linens fit well with kitchen treatments.

For the ultimate easy-sew window treatment, hand-sewn rings attach a pair of French tea towels to a basic tension rod, *above left*. Here the tea towels are the perfect size for a sliding window in a youthful kitchen decorated in a mid-20th-century mood. The damask weave of the French tea towels contrasts as an elegant touch to the funky character of the hand-painted drawer fronts and backsplash. To get the best results from a tension rod, measure the opening and purchase a rod that matches the measurement as closely as possible.

Hinged swing rods, also called drapery cranes, allow four valance panels to address privacy concerns, *above right*. In this easy but effective treatment, the fabric panels are lined with matching fabric because the swing rods, detailed with bird and ball finials, open to the reverse side. For fullness that creates the ruffled header, the fabric yardage is triple the rod width. When the upper panels are opened, the lower ones create a cafe-curtain effect. At night, the four panels can be closed for privacy.

WINDOW-SIDE DINING. Arrange your breakfast or kitchen table by a window for fresh air and pleasant natural light. If you enjoy the view, minimize treatments to soft wisps that gently diffuse light without blocking the scene. When you need privacy or sun control during certain times of the day, include blinds, shades, or shutters that can be opened or closed as needed.

A luminous sheer fabric, updated with a tattersall check motif, takes on a contemporary tone for a sleek dining setting, *above*. With a range of designs and finishes, versatile sheers adapt to a variety of settings, such as this one where the window is the focal point. The black iron rod extends beyond the window so the panels, attached on rings, frame the view.

A variation on the basic valance and cafe curtains, this breakfast room treatment, *opposite,* pairs a double valance and shirred banded panels. The double valance features a flat, tailored fabric, attached at the top of the window trim, as background. In the foreground, a flirty pleated valance in a contrasting print hangs from a painted drapery rod supported by brackets. Acorn-style finials, painted to match, neatly finish. The background valance fabric bands the white used for the cafe curtains.

A decorative hand-painted cornice, crafted from plywood, sets a whimsical mood for casual dining, *above.* Based on the window dimensions, a kraft paper pattern allowed the scalloped tops to be cut with a band saw. For a loose, painterly effect, the plaid is hand-painted over penciled guide points, rather than being taped off. Appliquéd scallop edging repeats the motifs as playful accents for a pair of ready-made sheers hung on a standard rod. **See page 110 for how-to directions.**

OFFICE EASY. If you crave natural light and a refreshing view for your home office or desk area, design a window treatment that softens the scene without obscuring the outdoors. Base your treatment on the location of your work or study area, and on the degree of sun or glare control you need. Look for pale colors or natural textures that soothe and quiet the scene.

▌ Silk clothing scarves find new purpose as the ultimate quick and no-sew treatment, *above.* For the easiest-ever project, drapery clips attach the fashionable scarves to a black iron rod to add a touch of drama to the setting. Decorative finials add a polished finishing touch. Blocks of cool celadon green give the fashionably sheer scarves an outdoors feel appropriate to an office of white walls and pale natural wood. The light colors visually expand the small nook with a free, open feeling.

▌ Available in a variety of colors and motifs, accessory scarves from a clothing boutique or department store offer an alternative to ready-made drapery scarves. Scarves with abstract motifs, such as the hand-painted color blocks, *right,* imbue a setting with a contemporary mood. Neutrals or patterns such as stylized leaves are other possibilities for uncluttered office settings. Plain scarves also may be painted to emulate this look.

■ An angle bracket, *left*, supports and shapes an unlined Roman shade fashioned from a vintage French burlap sack found at a flea market. Installation slightly below the tops of the doors allows easy opening and closing.

■ Primarily decorative, the seed-sack Roman shades, *below*, reduce glare on the home office computer screen. The width of the sacks conveniently fits the width of the door glass. The weight and body of the sacks eliminate the need for additional lining for the shades. The motifs and French wording enhance the stylish office where an antique table substitutes for a desk and a slipcovered armless chair takes the place of a more traditional office chair. The wall coloring closely matches lettering on one sack. **See page 111 for how-to directions.**

decoratingideas

As with any decorating project, planning and preparation are the keys to successfully executed window treatments. Before you start a project and buy supplies, ask yourself the following questions: What do you want the window treatment to accomplish—privacy, sun control, or the finishing touch to your room? Will the window treatment be the focal point or a subtle backdrop for other furnishings?

Do you want a treatment that adds color and frames the window? Or, is privacy your chief concern? Will you incorporate other fabric or furnishing changes, such as new table skirts or accent pillows? What is your budget for fabric and supplies? Does the treatment require sewing? If so, do your skills match the project? For example, each featured project has been created with time and skill estimates. Some projects require only basic hand-sewing skills. Others require a sewing machine and beginner skills; several projects for

lined window treatments or shades require intermediate sewing skills. If you prefer not to sew your own, local fabric stores and fabric outlets may offer lists of experienced seamstresses who can accomplish such projects. Whether you plan to sew your own treatments, work with a professional seamstress, or adapt ready-made ones, such as panels or window scarves, precise window measurements are crucial to the project.

MEASURING WINDOWS: Accurate measurements ensure attractive, properly sized window treatments—whether you are sewing a project from scratch or embellishing a ready-made treatment. Exact measurement is particularly important if you order roller or fabric shades to decorate as part of your project. Keep the following tips in mind:

1. **For the most exact measurements,** use a steel measuring tape. Decide whether you want your treatments to fit inside the window or to cover the window (an outside mount). Measure accordingly.

2. **For an inside mount,** measure the opening width at the top, middle, and bottom, recording the narrowest measurement. Do the same for the length, recording the longest measurement. Round to the closest ⅛ inch.

3. **For an outside mount,** measure the opening width, and add at least 3 inches to each side of the window opening if space allows. Measure the opening length, and add at least 2 inches in height for hardware and any overlap.

4. **To measure the drop for draperies,** measure your windows from where you install the rod to where you want the draperies to fall. For width, measure the full length of the rod. To calculate the length of a decorative scarf or a single fabric piece, measure the distance from the bottom of the drapery ring or the top of the rod to the desired length of the scarf. Multiply that measurement by 2, and add 10 inches to each side if you want the fabric to puddle on the floor. Measure the width of the area to be covered, and add that figure to the length for the total needed yardage.

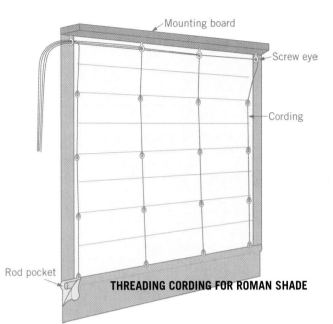

Mounting board

Screw eye

Cording

Rod pocket

THREADING CORDING FOR ROMAN SHADE

window basics projects

WINDOW TREATMENTS BASIC SUPPLY LIST

Shop fabric stores and outlets or discount stores that carry fabric and sewing supplies for basic items. Home centers and hardware stores are sources for the hammer, nails, drill, bits, and measuring tapes used in some projects. To help your project go as smoothly as possible, stock the following in addition to specific items listed under each project's supply list:

- Drill and bits
- Embroidery needle
- Glue for fabric, wood and general white glue
- Hammer
- Iron
- Ironing board
- Permanent marking pen
- Ruler
- Sewing machine or serger
- Sewing thread
- Sharp cutting shears, crafts knife
- Staple gun
- Steel measuring tape
- Straightedge
- Straight pins
- Tailor's chalk or pencil
- Tracing paper, newsprint, or brown poster paper
- Water-soluble marking pen

ROMAN SHADE, INSIDE MOUNT

SKILL LEVEL
Advanced

TIME
Several days

SUPPLIES FOR ONE

- Face fabric
- White or ivory lining fabric
- $\frac{3}{8}$-inch metal rod, about 1 inch shorter than the finished shade width
- $\frac{1}{2}$-inch-diameter plastic rings (or Roman shade ring tape)
- Clear nylon thread (optional)
- 1×2 wood strip, $\frac{1}{4}$ to $\frac{1}{2}$ inch shorter than the width of your window (for the mounting board)
- Adhesive nylon hook-and-loop tape
- Screw eyes large enough for multiple cording lengths
- Screws or two L-brackets with screws
- Nylon cording
- Awning cleat

ROMAN SHADE, INSIDE MOUNT

CUTTING THE FABRICS. Referring to the "Measuring Windows" section, page 81, measure the inside window width and length. This is the finished size of the shade.

- **Add 5 inches to the width and 10½ inches to the length.** Note: If you plan to hand-sew individual rings to the shade, add about ¾ inch for every 36 inches of fabric width and length to the measurements. This accommodates fabric taken up when stitching the rings in place.

- **Cut a rectangle with these measurements from the face fabric.** Cut the lining fabric, making it 3 inches narrower and 2½ inches longer than the finished size of the shade. Note: If you need to piece the shade fabric and lining, piece them identically. It is best to plan a seam where rings (or ring tape) will be attached. See "Attaching the Rings" on page 83.

SEWING THE SHADE. Place the face fabric and lining together with right sides facing; align the top edges and one side. Stitch along the side using a ½-inch seam allowance. Now align the opposite sides (the face fabric is wider than the lining). Stitch this seam. Press both seams open. Turn the shade right side out. Center the lining on the back of the shade and press.

- **At the top edge,** press under ½ inch, then 2 inches. Stitch in place. Press under 4 inches at the bottom of shade. Stitch across the width of the shade 1½ inches from the fold to create a rod pocket. Fold up the bottom another 4 inches. Stitch across width near the top fold. Insert the metal rod in the pocket, slip-stitch closed.

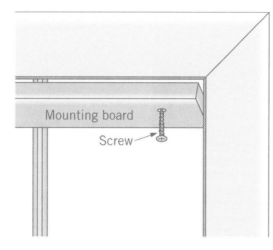

INSIDE MOUNT FOR ROMAN SHADE

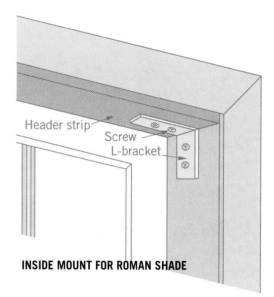

INSIDE MOUNT FOR ROMAN SHADE

ATTACHING THE RINGS. Mark the placement of rings on the wrong side of the shade, using a water-soluble marking pen. Place the first and last vertical rows about 2 inches from the sides. Plan the top horizontal row 4 inches from the top. Plan the bottom horizontal row just above the metal rod pocket. Position the rings 9 to 11 inches apart horizontally and 6 to 8 inches apart vertically. Using thread that matches the shade fabric or clear nylon thread, hand-sew the rings in place through both the face fabric and the lining. Or pin ring tape to the back as follows. Place the bottom ring of the tape just above the rod pocket. End with the top ring 4 inches from the top of the shade. Make sure the rings are perfectly aligned; then stitch around the tape.

PREPARING THE MOUNTING BOARD. Paint the mounting board to match your window frame, or cover it with lining fabric.

■ **Press one side of the hook-and-loop fastening tape** across the front edge of the mounting board, and the other side of the tape across the top edge on the wrong side of the shade. To mount the shade to the mounting board, press the hook-and-loop fastening tape together.

■ **Next, mark points on the underside of the mounting board** for the placement of screw eyes. The screw eyes must correspond with the vertical row of rings on the shade. Screw the screw eyes to each point.

THREADING THE RINGS. Cut the nylon cording into lengths that measure the length of a vertical row of rings, plus the width of the shade, plus at least half the length of a vertical row of rings.

Cut one length for each vertical row of rings.

■ **Knot the end of a cord length to the bottom ring of each vertical row.** Thread the first (left side) cord length through its vertical row of rings and the corresponding screw eye.

■ **Thread the next cording length through its vertical row of rings**, its corresponding screw eye, and then the screw eye to its left.

■ **Thread the remaining cording lengths** in the same manner in order as directed above, threading each length through all of the screw eyes to the left. When all threading is complete, all cording lengths should be threaded through the far-left screw eye. Tie the excess lengths together in a loose knot.

MOUNTING THE SHADE. Secure the mounting board inside the window to the top of the window frame. You can screw it directly to the top of the frame or secure it with two L-brackets.

■ **Mount the awning cleat to the right of the window.** Pull on the cording lengths to make sure the shade pulls up evenly; then release the shade. Braid the cording lengths together, and knot them at the end. Wrap the braided length around the awning cleat to hold the shade at the desired level.

ROMAN SHADE, OUTSIDE MOUNT

■ **Use the materials list and follow the instructions above**, except for the following adjustments.

■ **For an outside mount,** measure the opening width, and add at least 3 inches to each side of the window opening if space allows. After you

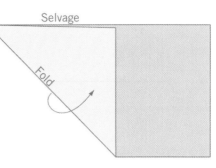

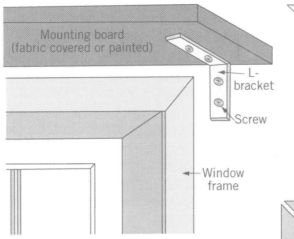

OUTSIDE MOUNT FOR ROMAN SHADE

TO MAKE PIPING, FIRST FIND BIAS LINE

CAREFULLY MEASURE AND CUT STRIPS

POSITION AT RIGHT ANGLE AND SEAM STRIPS

TURN AND PRESS CASING FOR PIPING

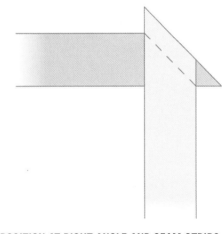

SEW THROUGH CASING CLOSE TO CORDING

SELF-COVERED PIPING SUPPLIES FOR ONE WINDOW
(IN ADDITION TO THE BASIC SUPPLY LIST)

- Fabric
- Rotary cutter, rotary-cutter ruler, and self-healing mat
- Cording
- Zipper foot

have prepared the mounting board, temporarily secure it to the wall above the window frame using two L-brackets. Then take the length measurement for the shade, beginning at the top edge of the mounting board. These measurements are the finished size of the shade.

SELF-COVERED PIPING

CUTTING THE FABRIC. Establish the bias grain of the fabric. To do this, first "square up" the fabric so the corners are at 45-degree angles. Fold one selvage (vertical side) up to meet the top crosswise (horizontal) edge. See the diagram. Press the diagonal fold, then open it up. Cut along the diagonal.

■ **Use the rotary cutter, ruler, and mat to cut** fabric strips the desired width, cutting them parallel to the diagonal cut. See the diagram.

JOINING THE STRIPS. With right sides facing, place two strips at right angles, matching the ¼-inch seam lines. (The ends should overlap.) See the diagram. Sew strips together. Continue adding strips until the pieced length is as long as the cording. Turn and press casing strip.

COVERING THE CORDING. Fold the pieced length around the cording with wrong sides facing and the raw edges aligned. Stitch close to the cording using a zipper foot attachment on the sewing machine.

LIVING ROOM TOPPER
SKILL LEVEL
Beginner
TIME
2 hours
SUPPLIES FOR ONE
- Hanging rod with finials and mounting hardware
- Floral-print fabric
- White or ivory lining fabric
- 2½-inch-wide braid-and-tassel trim
- Two 1-yard lengths of ½-inch-diameter cord with 7-inch tassels

LIVING ROOM SHEERS
SKILL LEVEL
Beginner
TIME
2 hours
SUPPLIES FOR ONE
- Wrought-iron drapery rod with mounting hardware
- Sheer pale green leaf-print fabric
- Two cup hooks
- Four plastic curtain rings

LIVING ROOM TOPPER
(PROJECT SHOWN ON PAGES 8–10)
- **Mount the hanging rod** above the window.
- **For the fabric width,** measure the hanging rod, and multiply by 2¼. The fabric depth, excluding trims, is 26 inches.
- **Cut one rectangle with these measurements** from the floral-print fabric and another from lining fabric. With right sides facing and using a ½-inch seam allowance, sew the rectangles together; leave an opening for turning in the center of one edge. Clip corners, turn right side out, and press. Sew the opening closed.
- **Topstitch the braid-and-tassel trim** to the short sides and one long side, mitering the trim at the corners.
- **Drape the swag over the hanging rod,** securing it in the corners with a tasseled cord.
NO-SEW TIP: Instead of sewing the braid-and-tassel trim to the swag, glue it in place with fabric glue.

LIVING ROOM SHEERS
(PROJECT SHOWN ON PAGES 8–10)
- **Mount the drapery rod** to the window.
- **For the sheer width,** measure the rod, and multiply by 1½; add 3 inches for ¾-inch (doubled) side hems. For the length, measure from the rod to the floor, and add 2½ inches for the rod casing and 8 inches for the bottom (doubled) hem. The tieback measurement is 11×19 inches.
- **Cut out two sheers and two tiebacks from the leaf-print fabric.** If you need to piece the drape, place a full fabric width in the center with narrower widths on the sides. Use ½-inch seam allowances to piece fabrics together. Press seams open.
- **To sew each sheer,** press under 4 inches twice on the bottom edge. Hand- or machine-stitch in place. Press under ¾ inch, twice on each side, and stitch. Press under ½ inch then 2 inches at the top for the casing; stitch a scant 2 inches from the top. Slip the sheers onto the curtain rod.
- **For each tieback,** fold the rectangle in half crosswise with right sides facing. The shape should measure 5½×19 inches. Using a ½-inch seam allowance, stitch the three open edges, leaving an opening for turning right side out in the long edge. Clip the corners and turn right side out. Press; then sew the opening closed. Sew a ring to each top corner.
- **Screw a cup hook into the wall,** and loop the tieback rings over the hook.
NO-SEW TIPS: 1. Instead of spending tedious hours hand-sewing hems, use iron-on tape to finish the work in minutes. **2.** Use ribbon or tasseled cording for tiebacks.

CAFE SHEER
SKILL LEVEL
Beginner
TIME
1 hour
SUPPLIES FOR ONE
- Wrought-iron drapery rod with mounting hardware
- Sheer pale green leaf-print fabric

CAFE SHEER
(PROJECT SHOWN ON PAGES 8 AND 10–11)

- **Mount the rod to the window.**

- **To determine the sheer's width,** measure the rod, and multiply by $2\frac{1}{2}$. To this measurement add 3 inches for $\frac{3}{4}$-inch (doubled) side hems. For the length, measure from the rod to the floor, and add $2\frac{1}{2}$ inches for the rod casing and 8 inches for the bottom (doubled) hem. Cut sheer from leaf-print fabric. Note: If you need to piece the sheer, place a full fabric width in the center with narrower widths on the sides, and join with French seams.

- **Sew the cafe sheer as directed** for the living room sheers.

DINING ROOM DRAPERIES

SKILL LEVEL
Intermediate
TIME
2 hours
SUPPLIES FOR ONE
- Wrought-iron hanging rod with finials and mounting hardware
- Damask fabric for face fabric and tieback
- Ivory cotton for lining
- 1-inch-wide red cotton fringe, the length of the finished drape
- Six wrought-iron rings
- Six curtain hooks (to attach rings)
- Two plastic curtain rings
- One cup hook

DINING ROOM DRAPERIES
(PROJECT SHOWN ON PAGE 12)

- **In order to take accurate measurements for the drapery,** first mount the hanging rod.
- For the drapery width, measure the rod, and multiply by 2½. Add 5 inches for 2½-inch side hems. For the length, measure from the rod to the floor. Add several inches to this measurement if you want the draperies to softly puddle on the floor. Add 4½ inches for the top hem and 8 inches for the bottom (doubled) hem.
The tieback measurement is 9×36 inches.
- **For the lining width,** measure the rod and multiply by 2½. Then subtract 3 inches. For the length, add 3 inches to the finished drapery length (do not include top and bottom hem measurements).
- **Using a water-soluble marking pen and straightedge,** mark the measurements for the drapery and tieback on damask and the lining on cotton.
Cut out the pieces. Note: If you need to piece the drapery and lining, place a full fabric width in the center with narrower widths on the sides. Use ½-inch seam allowances to piece fabrics together.
- **To hem the drapery,** first press under 4 inches twice on the bottom edge. Hand- or machine-stitch in place. Press under 2½ inches on each side. Press under ½ inch, and then 4 inches at the top.
- **To prepare the lining,** press under 2 inches twice for the bottom hem. Hand- or machine-stitch.
- **Working on a flat surface,** place the lining on

top of the drape with the right sides facing. Position the top edges even, centering the lining. **Note:** The bottom of the lining should be 1 inch from the bottom of the drapery, and the lining should be 1½ inches from each side.
- **Open up the pressed hems on the drapery** (the sides and top). Pin sides of drapery and lining together with edges even and right sides facing. Sew sides using ½-inch seam allowances. Turn right side out. Turn down the top edge and hem.
- **Sew the fringe to one side** of the drapery.
- **Attach the wrought-iron rings** to the drapery with the drape hooks. Slip the drapery on the rod.
- **Check the tieback length around the drapery,** adjusting its length as necessary. Fold the strip in half lengthwise with right sides facing. Using a ½-inch seam allowance, stitch the three open edges, leaving an opening (for turning right side out) in the long edge. Clip the corners and turn right side out. Press; then sew the opening closed. Sew a plastic ring to each top corner.
- **Screw a cup hook into the wall** and loop the tieback rings over the hook.

MASTER BEDROOM ROMAN SHADE
SKILL LEVEL
Advanced
TIME
5 hours per shade
SUPPLIES FOR ONE
- See page 82.
- Cedar green-and-gold stripe satin fabric
- White or ivory lining fabric
- 2-inch-wide bronze-and-metallic gold tasseled braid trim

BEDROOM SHEERS
FOR FRENCH DOORS
AND WINDOW
SKILL LEVEL
Beginner
TIME
2 hours
SUPPLIES FOR ONE
- ¼-inch-diameter brass rods with mounting hardware (two for each door, one or two for each window)
- Bronze-colored lace
- Bronze gimp (to edge the sides of each panel)

MASTER BEDROOM ROMAN SHADE
(PROJECT SHOWN ON PAGES 12–13)
- **Follow the general instructions on page 82–84** with the following additions.
- **For the valance pattern,** draw a rectangle on tracing paper that measures 8 inches tall by the width of the mounting board, minus 4 inches (allowance for braid trim). Mark the center on the bottom edge of the rectangle. Draw a gentle arc from the center to one top corner; then make a mirror image on the other side. Adjust curve as necessary. Add the depth of the mounting board to the top edge. Add ½ inch for seam allowances around the curved edge. Cut out the pattern.
- **Cut one pattern from the face fabric** and one from the lining. With right sides facing, sew the two fabrics together, leaving an opening along the straight edge for turning. Clip the curve and the corners. Turn right side out and press. Topstitch across the opening.
- **Pin the braid trim to the curved edge,** omitting mounting board allowance. Topstitch in place.
- **Before proceeding** to the "Mounting the Shade" section in the general instructions, page 83, add the valance. Use a staple gun to secure the untrimmed mounting board allowance to the top of the mounting board. Then proceed with the general instructions.

FOR THE FRENCH DOORS. The French door shades are made just like the window shades with the following exceptions: The mounting boards are exterior mounts, and the shades cover the entire door width.

BEDROOM SHEERS
(PROJECT SHOWN ON PAGE 12)
FOR THE FRENCH DOORS. Mount the rods inside each French door, at the top and bottom.
- **Measure the door width and the length from rod to rod.** Add ¾ inch to the width for ⅜-inch seam allowances. Add 6 inches to the length for (triple-turned) rod pockets. Cut a rectangle.
- **On each side, press ⅜ inch to the right side of the lace panel.** Baste in place. Press under 1 inch three times at the top of the panel. Stitch across the inside fold to form a rod pocket. Repeat for the bottom of the panel.
- **Topstitch gimp over side seam allowances,** covering raw edges. Do not stitch over pockets.
FOR THE WINDOW. To make an interior-mounted Roman shade with sheers, mount mounting board for the shade before mounting the brass rod(s).
- **Stitch and mount the sheer** as directed for the French door sheers. Or leave the bottom of the window sheer unattached. Instructions follow.
- **Mount the rod to the top of the window.** Measure the window width, and add ¾ inch for ⅜-inch seam allowances. Measure the window length from the rod to the sill. Add 3 inches for a (triple-turned) rod pocket and 3½ inches for a hem. Cut a rectangle from lace.
- **Hem the sides, and make a top rod pocket.**
- **Press under ½ inch,** then 3 inches for a bottom hem. Blindstitch the hem.
- **Starting just below the rod pocket and ending at the bottom of the hem,** topstitch gimp over the seam allowance on each side, covering edges.

GIRL'S BEDROOM ROMAN SHADES FOR FRENCH DOORS

SKILL LEVEL

Advanced

TIME

4 hours per shade

SUPPLIES FOR ONE

- See page 82.
- Cotton print fabric
- White or ivory lining fabric
- Ball fringe
- Bias tape (to edge the ball fringe)

KITCHEN NOOK VALANCE

SKILL LEVEL

Beginner

TIME

1 hour

SUPPLIES FOR ONE

- ½-inch-square hanging rod with finials and mounting hardware
- Fruit-print fabric for face fabric
- Ivory cotton fabric for lining
- Coordinating print for border

GIRL'S BEDROOM ROMAN SHADES FOR FRENCH DOORS

(PROJECT SHOWN ON PAGE 14)

- **Follow the general instructions on pages 82–84.**
- **Cover the edge of the ball fringe with bias tape.** Glue the fringe ends to the back of the shade. Let the fringe scallop to give it the look of a valance.

KITCHEN NOOK VALANCE

(PROJECT SHOWN ON PAGE 15)

- **Mount the hanging rod above the window.**
- **For width,** measure rod, and multiply by 2.
- **The valance depth at the ends is 17½ inches.** On tracing paper pieced to fit, draw a rectangle that measures 17½ inches by the valance width. Fold rectangle in half crosswise to find the center. Measure down 9½ inches from the center top, and mark this Point A. Mark both bottom corners Point B. Draw a gentle arc from one Point B to Point A. Make a mirror image of the arc on the opposite side, adjusting the curve as needed. Add ½ inch for seam allowances. Cut out the pattern.
- **Cut one pattern each from print** and lining.
- **Pin the lining to the fruit-print valance** with right sides facing. Mark a dot on each short side 1½ inches from the top edge. Draw a second dot on each short side 3 inches from the top edge. (These marks are for the rod casing.)
- **With ½-inch seam allowances,** sew the pieces together, leaving seam unstitched between dots and leaving opening for turning. Clip corners, turn right side out, and press. Hand-sew opening.
- **With a water-soluble marker,** draw a line between dots for casing. Machine-stitch on lines.
- **From the coordinating print,** cut 2-inch-wide strips on diagonal, and join into a length slightly longer than curved edge. Press under ¼ inch on one short edge and ½ inch on the long edges.
- **Pin the border strip to the bottom edge** of the valance, trimming away the excess at the unpressed edge, except for ¼ inch. Turn under the ¼ inch. Topstitch the border to the valance.

DINING ROOM PANELS
SKILL LEVEL
Beginner
TIME
2 hours
SUPPLIES FOR ONE
- 1¼-inch-diameter wood rod (painted white) with mounting hardware
- 54-inch-wide taupe and peach silk fabrics
- Antique tiebacks (to use decoratively as finials)

BREAKFAST ROOM VALANCE
SKILL LEVEL
Beginner
TIME
2 hours
SUPPLIES FOR ONE
- ½-inch-diameter wood hanging rod (painted white) with finials and mounting hardware
- Loosely woven linen fabric
- Bits of new or vintage lace
- Vintage shell buttons
- Small tassels

DINING ROOM PANELS
(PROJECT SHOWN ON PAGE 18)
- **Mount the wood hanging rod.**
- **Each panel width is the width of the silk fabric (54 inches).** The bottom peach band is 40½ inches tall, including a 1-inch seam allowance, extra fabric for puddling on the floor, and 3½ inches for the hem. The top taupe panel is 62½ inches tall, including a 1-inch seam allowance and 8½ inches for the rod pocket and shirred top. Measure your window and adapt measurements accordingly. Cut fabric for two panels.
- **For each panel,** sew the two contrasting pieces together with a 1-inch seam and right sides facing. To finish the seam, press the seam allowance to the peach side. Trim the peach seam allowance to ¼ inch. Press under the taupe seam allowance twice, hiding the trimmed allowance. Topstitch in place.
- **Press under ¼ inch twice on the sides, and stitch.** Press under ½ inch, then 8 inches at the top. Stitch close to the bottom fold; then sew 4 inches from the bottom fold for the rod casing.
- **For the bottom hem,** press under ½ inch, then 3 inches. Stitch in place.
- **Gather panels on the rod.** Hang and attach decorative tiebacks or finials.

BREAKFAST ROOM VALANCE
(PROJECT SHOWN ON PAGE 19)
- **Mount the wood hanging rod.**
- **The length of the finished valance is 21 inches.** Adapt the length to your window, if necessary. To the finished length measurement, add ½ inch for a rolled hem and 5½ inches for the rod pocket and shirred top. For the width, measure the window width, and multiply by 1½ or 2; and add 1 inch for rolled side hems. Cut a fabric rectangle with these measurements.
- **Press under doubled ¼-inch hems** on the sides, and hand- or machine-sew. Repeat for the bottom hem.
- **At the top edge, press under ½ inch,** then 5½ inches. Machine-stitch close to the bottom fold. Then stitch 2½ inches from the bottom fold to create a 2½-inch rod casing.
- **Hand-sew evenly spaced trims,** such as lace, buttons, and tassels, along the edge.

BAY WINDOW PANELS
SKILL LEVEL
Intermediate
TIME
4 hours
SUPPLIES FOR ONE
- Decorative hanging rod with mounting hardware and clip-on rings
- 1½ yards of 54-inch-wide cream fabric (per panel)
- 2½ yards of 54-inch-wide mocha fabric (per panel)
- 3½ yards of lining (per panel)
- 1½ yards of 2-inch-wide mocha fringe (per panel)
- Serger or sewing machine
- Hook-and-loop fastening tape (for tieback fastening)

BAY WINDOW PANELS
(PROJECT SHOWN ON PAGE 23)

- **Mount the hanging rod above the window frame.**
- **Each panel is one fabric width wide by the finished length of the window plus puddle.** The featured panels are 124 inches long, made from 19-, 54-, and 64-inch bands. Measurements include seam allowances and hems.
- **With right sides facing, pin bands together.** Serge with a serger sewing machine that has a ½-inch overlocking stitch; or sew on a regular sewing machine using a ½-inch seam allowance. Press under a 2-inch bottom hem twice, and topstitch. Topstitch fringe to top of the bottom mocha layer.
- **Cut drapery lining fabric 4 inches shorter than the hemmed panel** (the width will be cut later). Press under 1 inch twice for the bottom hem, and topstitch. Set aside.
- **Press under double 1½-inch side hems on the front panel.** Do not stitch. Cut lining width the same width as the front panel (from folded edge to folded edge).
- **Open up the pressed side seams.** Pin right sides of front panel and lining together at one side, matching the hemmed edges. Note: The lining will be much narrower and shorter. Stitch from the bottom hem to the top, using wide, 1½-inch seam allowances.
- **Turn right side out,** centering the lining on the back of the panel, and press. Press under 3 inches twice at the top of the panel to the lining side. Pin and stitch through all layers near the

bottom fold to create a rod pocket, or stitch as a top band shown above.
- **Add clips at regular intervals,** clipping adjacent panels together.
- **Cut a 5-inch-wide length of cream fabric for a tieback.** Fold strip in half lengthwise with right sides facing. Stitch open edges, leaving an opening for turning. Clip corners, turn right side out, and press. Slip-stitch opening closed. Attach small pieces of hook-and-loop fastening tape to the ends. Secure around the panel just above the decorative fringe.

LIGHT AND PRIVACY PIECED PANELS

SKILL LEVEL

Intermediate

TIME

3 hours

SUPPLIES FOR ONE

- Hanging rod and mounting hardware
- Two contrasting fabrics for each panel
- Serger
- Drapery weights

CONTRAST PANELS

SKILL LEVEL

Intermediate

TIME

2 to 3 hours

SUPPLIES FOR ONE

- Four full-length ready-made tabbed panels sized for windows
- 3 yards of contrasting fabric

LIGHT AND PRIVACY PIECED PANELS
(PROJECT SHOWN ON PAGE 22)

- **Mount the rod several inches above the window frame.**
- **The pieced panels shown on page 22 are 99 inches long with seven separate sections.** The taupe sections are 11 inches long (finished). The pale blue sections vary in length. From top to bottom, they measure 14, 17, 21, and 28 inches long (finished). Adjust lengths and determine the panel widths to suit your window.
- **When planning fabric amounts,** add 1 inch to sections two through six for ½-inch seam allowances. Add 3½ inches to the top pale blue sections for doubled 1½-inch rod pockets and a seam allowance. Add 6½ inches to each bottom pale blue section for doubled 3-inch hems and a seam allowance.
- **Pin, then stitch sections together,** alternating colors. Press seams open. Serge sides from top to bottom; then press under the ½-inch seam allowance, and hand-tack the entire length. Press under a doubled 1½-inch rod pocket at the tops. Stitch close to the bottom fold. Press under a doubled 3-inch hem at the bottoms. Insert the drapery weights, and sew the hem.

CONTRAST PANELS
(PROJECT SHOWN ON PAGE 24)

- **Remove all tabs** by clipping threads with small, sharp scissors or with a seam cutter. Restitch opening with straight machine stitches.
- **Remove seams on both sides** and the bottom hem of two panels. Stitch the two panels together to make one large panel.
- **Measure the length of the large panel** at both sides, and add 1 inch to each. Cut a 4-inch-wide strip from contrasting fabric to each length measurement.
- **Stitch a doubled ¼-inch hem** along one long edge and the short edges of each strip. Stitch the other long edge to the contrasting panel using a ½-inch seam allowance. Cut a 7-inch contrasting band to fit the bottom width of the large panel plus 1 inch. Stitch a doubled ¼-inch hem along one long edge and the short edges. Stitch the remaining edge to the bottom of the panel with a ½-inch seam allowance.
- **For side panels,** repeat the above steps. Contrast is added to only the inside edges and the bottom as shown. Cut and stitch three contrasting tiebacks with the remaining scrap fabric.

ROD-POCKET SHEERS
SKILL LEVEL
Intermediate
TIME
2 hours
SUPPLIES FOR ONE
- 1-inch-diameter drapery rod and mounting hardware
- Plain sheer fabric for the face panel
- Patterned sheer fabric for the lining panel

CASEMENT PANEL
SKILL LEVEL
Beginner
TIME
1 hour
SUPPLIES FOR ONE
- ½-inch-diameter hanging rod with mounting hardware
- Blue-and-white-striped fabric
- 1-inch-deep beaded trim (cut the length 1 inch longer than the finished width of the panel)

ROD-POCKET SHEERS
(PROJECT SHOWN ON PAGE 25)
- **Mount the drapery rod.**
- **Measure the width of the window from frame to frame, and divide by 2.** Add 1 inch for ½-inch seam allowances. These panels used the full yardage width for especially soft gathers. For fuller gathers, multiply the width by 1½, 2, or 2½, and piece the panels.
- **Measure the length from the drapery rod to the floor.** Add 3½ inches for a 2-inch ruffled header, seam allowance, and hem. Cut two panels from each sheer fabric to these measurements.
- **Carefully pin a plain and patterned panel together** with right sides facing.
- **Serge the side seams together from bottom to top,** stopping 4½ inches from the top for the rod pocket. Use a serger or a sewing machine to sew the seams separately for the next 2 inches. Sew the remaining 2½ inches together, then sew across the top with a ½-inch seam allowance.
- **Turn the curtains right side out.** Press under serged areas at rod pocket. Stitch a 2-inch-wide rod pocket, starting 2 inches from the top edge. Press under ½ inch twice for separate hems, and stitch.

CASEMENT PANEL
(PROJECT SHOWN ON PAGE 27)
- **Mount the hanging rod to the window.**
- **Measure the width of the window, and add 1 inch.** Measure the length from the hanging rod to the bottom of the window, and add 1 inch. Cut a rectangle with these measurements from the fabric. Note: The beading will hang about ¾ inch below the bottom of the window.
- **Press under a double ¼-inch hem at the sides.** Topstitch in place. Press under a double ¼-inch hem at the bottom edge. Pin the beading to the bottom edge, turning under the ends. Stitch in place.
- **For the rod pocket,** press under the top edge ¼ inch, then ¾ inch. Topstitch close to the bottom fold. Slip the panel onto the hanging rod.

**SHEER ROMAN
SHADE
SKILL LEVEL**
Intermediate
TIME
5 hours per shade
SUPPLIES FOR ONE
- See page 82.
- Sheer fabric for
shade and lining
- Sewing machine
(serger or regular
with zigzag-stitch
attachment)
- Wood dowel, 1-inch
wider than shade
width (instead of
metal rod)

**BEADED
EMBELLISHMENT
SKILL LEVEL**
Beginner
TIME
1 hour (several hours if
you hand-sew trim)
SUPPLIES FOR ONE
- Ready-made tabbed,
sheer panel
- Beaded trim
- Washable fabric glue
- Four glass drawer
knobs

SHEER ROMAN SHADE
(PROJECT SHOWN ON PAGE 24)
CUTTING THE FABRIC. These shades are cut
almost 2½ times the height of the window.
This allows the shades to be mounted above the
window casing and for permanent pleats at the
bottom hem. Note: These windows are 30 inches
long. The fabric is cut 72 inches long. (This
includes fabric for a rod pocket and seams.) Plan
height of your panels accordingly.
- **Cut the face fabric and lining 1 inch wider than
the finished window width** and to length.
SEWING THE SHADE. Carefully pin face fabric and
lining together with right sides facing. Serge sides,
then across the bottom. Turn right side out, and
press. Pin around the edges to keep the fabric in
place. Press under 1 inch at the top, and stitch.
ATTACHING THE RINGS. Mark a dot on lining
side 6 inches up from the bottom edge and 2
inches in from one side. Repeat for other side.
(Two rows of rings are used.) Sew other rings
vertically at 8-inch intervals to top of shade and
2 inches in from sides. Attach rings with
stationary zigzag stitch or hand-sew in place.
- **Make a small rod pocket by folding 2 inches of
the shade together** at the bottom horizontal row
of rings. Pin pocket flat to lining with rings facing
out. Stitch, creating a 1-inch rod pocket.
- **Tightly tie first three rows of rings together at
the bottom** to form permanent pleats in shade.
Insert dowel.
- **Prepare the mounting board,** thread the rings,
and mount the shade for an exterior mount
following the general instructions on page 83.

BEADED EMBELLISHMENT
(PROJECT SHOWN ON PAGE 27)
- **Measure the length and width of one ready-
made panel.** Multiply the length by 2,
and add the width. Divide this number by 36.
This is the bead trim yardage needed.
- **Pin the trim in place, starting at the bottom
edge,** pivoting at the top corners, and ending at
the opposite bottom edge. Attach the trim with
fabric glue, or whipstitch the trim in place,
keeping the tension of the stitches even.
Note: Use the glue sparingly on sheer fabrics,
and test a small area before attaching the entire
beaded length. Hand-sewing may give better
results on very sheer fabrics.
- **Drill small holes in the window molding to
receive the drawer knobs.** Screw knobs into
molding, and hang the panel.

GARDEN-STYLE

SKILL LEVEL

Beginner

TIME

1 hour

SUPPLIES FOR ONE

- Sheer fabric
- Three small brass rings
- Two custom-made iron bird spikes for mounting hardware
- One package of natural raffia
- One small tree branch for curtain rod

GARDEN-STYLE DECORATING

(PROJECT SHOWN ON PAGES **28, 29, 34, 35**)

- **Measure the window width, including any molding trim, and add 1 inch for hems.** Measure the window length in the same way. Cut the sheer fabric to these measurements.
- **Press under ¼-inch twice on all four edges of the fabric panel,** and stitch by hand or machine. Sew a brass ring at each top corner and in the top center of the fabric.
- **Drill a hole at each edge of the window frame, and secure the bird spikes.** Hang the branch on the spike (see the photo detail, page 35).
- **Slip a full length of raffia through each brass ring,** then tie the curtain to the branch.

SIMPLE SOPHISTICATION (PANELS)

(PROJECT SHOWN ON PAGE **31**)

- **Mount the hanging rod.**
- **Cut two 54×97-inch panels from the print fabric.** From the solid-color fabric, cut two 13×97-inch border strips and two 9×18-inch tieback strips. **Note:** All measurements include ½ inch for seam allowances.
- **On the right side of each panel,** reinforce the top edge with a narrow strip of iron-on interfacing.
- **Press under ½ inch on one long edge of the border strip.** With right sides facing and matching raw edges, pin the border strip to the inside edge of one panel. Stitch the bottom seam, the side seam, then the top seam. Turn right side out. Press under ½ inch across the remainder of the top edge and the bottom edge, and topstitch.
- **Turn 4 inches of the border strip edge to the right side of the panel.** Fold over two more times, creating a solid-color border. Tack the top edge 2 inches from the new outer edge. Turn the opposite side 4 inches twice to the wrong side of the panel, and tack as before.
- **Pin five evenly spaced 1½-inch deep folds of fabric across the top of each panel to create single pleats.** Tack the pleats with a few straight stitches by hand or machine.
- **To hang the panel,** sew seven evenly spaced rings to the top edge.
- **Fold each tieback strip in half lengthwise with right sides facing.** Stitch ends and side, leaving an opening along the side. Clip corners, turn right side out, and press. Slip-stitch opening closed. Sew rings to top corners. Hang on cup hooks.

SIMPLE (PANELS)

SKILL LEVEL

Intermediate

TIME

3 hours

SUPPLIES FOR ONE

- Iron hanging rod, rings, and hardware
- 5½ yards of 54-inch-wide sheer print fabric
- 9½ yards of 54-inch-wide solid-color fabric
- Narrow iron-on interfacing strips
- Four small plastic rings for tiebacks
- Two cup hooks

SIMPLE SOPHISTICATION (SCARF)
SKILL LEVEL
Intermediate
TIME
1 hour
SUPPLIES FOR ONE
■ Drapery rods and mounting hardware
■ 196-inch ready-made drapery scarf

FRINGED PANELS
SKILL LEVEL
Beginner
TIME
3 hours
SUPPLIES FOR ONE
■ Drapery rod with finials and hardware
■ Two ready-made muslin panels
■ Four ready-made unlined houndstooth panels
■ Wooden curtain rings, painted black
■ 8 yards of 9-inch-wide bouillon fringe
■ 8 yards of 2½-inch-wide black trim

SIMPLE SOPHISTICATION (SCARF)
(PROJECT SHOWN ON PAGE 30)

■ **Mount drapery rods just below the crown molding.** Fold the scarf in half crosswise, and cut. Press under ½ inch, then 3 inches at the top of each panel for a rod pocket. Note: Make the pocket deeper, if necessary, to fit the drapery rod. Stitch close to the bottom fold.

■ **Make one 3-inch-wide (horizontal) buttonhole in each rod pocket** to accommodate hanging brackets. Install panels on rod.

DOUBLE THE IMPACT (FRINGED PANELS)
(PROJECT SHOWN ON PAGE 36)

■ **Mount the drapery rod just above the window.**

■ **Sew a muslin panel** between two houndstooth panels, using ½-inch seam allowances and sewing from the top to the bottom of the panels. If the panels don't align at the bottom, trim the edge even. Repeat with the remaining panels.

■ **Stitch curtain rings,** evenly spaced, to the back of the panels. Slip the panels on the rod, and check the length for the addition of trims. Shorten the panels, if necessary.

■ **Pin, then topstitch the fringe across the bottom edge.** Repeat with the 2½-inch-wide trim, placing it just above the fringe.

HEADSTART WITH READY-MADES
SKILL LEVEL
Intermediate
TIME
2 to 3 days
SUPPLIES FOR ONE
- Ready-made natural cotton canvas Roman shades and mounting hardware
- Newspaper and newsprint
- No. 8 round artist's brush
- Red fabric paint
- Plastic-foam plates
- Circle sponge (the size of a quarter)
- Large sponge (for tulip motif)
- Two swing rods with extra extension
- 8-inch-wide plain dressmaker's muslin
- Two ready-made olive sailcloth panels
- Off-white cording

HEADSTART WITH READY-MADES
(PROJECT SHOWN ON PAGES **32** AND **33**)

- **To paint the Roman shades,** cover the work surface with newspaper topped with sheets of newsprint. Decide on the scale of the grid. Using a straightedge, lightly draw guidelines. Make sure the grid will match if shades are painted for multiple windows.
- **Heavily load the artist's brush with paint, and paint the lines.** To detail intersections with circles, use a quarter-size circle sponge. Pour paint onto a plastic-foam plate, and work paint into sponge. Press firmly into fabric. Fill in with brushed-on paint as needed. Referring to the photograph, page 33, sponge circles and hand-paint small flowers in the center of the grid squares. Allow to dry; then mount in window. See page 82.
- **Mount the swing rods.**
- **To make panels,** cut four 10-inch-wide muslin strips to the length of the olive panels, plus 1 inch. Note: Finished panels are 8 inches wide.
- **Mark two of the panels with 1-inch-wide seam allowances.**
- **Draw or trace a thin,** stylized 10-inch-tall tulip shape onto paper. Cut out for a pattern. Trace shape onto a sponge, and cut out with scissors or a crafts knife.
- **Dip sponge into paint, and stamp tulips onto the two panels,** referring to the photograph for placement. Note: Be sure to stamp the panels so they are mirror images of each other. Hand-paint the vine and swirls to connect tulip pairs.

Fill in sponged tulips, as desired. Allow panels to thoroughly dry.
- **Heat-set the paint by ironing the reverse side for 30 seconds** at a temperature suitable for the fabric.
- **With right sides facing and using 1-inch seam allowances,** sew painted panels to the olive panels with cording between.
- **Press under one long edge on each remaining muslin (facing) panel.** With right sides facing and raw edges aligned, pin the facing to the painted panel. Mark for casing. Sew the top, bottom, and side, leaving the casing area open. Clip corners, turn right side out, and press. Stitch casing; then hand-sew facing in place.
- **Do not wash.** Dry-clean when necessary.

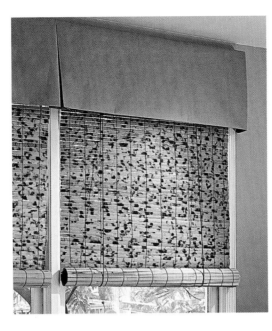

DOUBLE THE IMPACT (BAMBOO SHADE (WITH CORNICE)

SKILL LEVEL

Beginner

TIME

2 hours

SUPPLIES FOR ONE

- Bamboo shades to fit your window
- 30-inch-wide heavy brown kraft paper
- 1×2 wood board, 2 inches longer than the window frame width
- L-brackets
- Screws

SPELL IT OUT

SKILL LEVEL

Beginner/Intermediate

TIME

4 hours

SUPPLIES FOR ONE

- 45-inch-wide sheer striped fabric
- Bronze hand-hewn nails
- Brass letters or other decorative heading
- Vintage metal flowers with stems or an appropriate substitute

DOUBLE THE IMPACT (BAMBOO SHADE WITH KRAFT PAPER CORNICE)

(PROJECT SHOWN ON PAGE 37)

- **Measure your window.** (See page 81 for instructions.) Install the bamboo shade. Cut a length of kraft paper the width of the window frame plus 20 inches. Fold the paper in half lengthwise, making a sharp crease.
- **Fold a box pleat at the center of the paper length.** (Allow 2 inches in the center, then make the 1-inch folds). Using a staple gun, attach the top of the paper to the 2-inch side of the board, starting at the center and working out to each end.
- **Fold a pleat (as directed above) at each end of the board.** To ease the turn around the corners, make a light fold in the paper at the corners, then open up.
- **Fold down the entire length of paper with the stapled side on the top.** Wrap the paper around the ends, adjusting the corners on top of the board. Staple in back. Staple the sides to the top of the board.
- **Mount L-brackets above the window frame.** Attach the valance to the L-brackets with screws.

SPELL IT OUT

(PROJECT SHOWN ON PAGES 38–39)

Note: The vertical stripe of the fabric is used horizontally for the curtain band. From one side of the striped fabric, cut two 4-inch-wide bands the width of the window plus 1 inch (for 1/2-inch seam allowances).

- **Measure the window width, including the moldings, and divide in half.** Add 1 inch for doubled 1/4-inch seam allowances. This is the width for each window panel.
- **Measure the length from the top molding to the floor,** adding extra length if you want the panels to puddle on the floor. Add 1 inch for a seam allowance and a rolled hem. Cut two fabric panels with these measurements.
- **Press under 1/4 inch twice on the sides and bottom edge of the panels, and topstitch.**
- **With right sides facing and matching raw edges,** center and pin the band across the two panels. The band should extend 1/2 inch at each end. Stitch in place. Press the seam allowances toward the band.
- **Press under 1/2 inch on the bottom long edge of the remaining band.** With right sides facing and raw edges even, sew the bands together at the sides and top. Clip the corners, turn right side out, and press. Slip-stitch the opening closed.
- **Make small, evenly spaced buttonholes across the band.** Drill holes into the wall, just above the molding, and pound in nails. Hang curtain from nails through buttonholes. Gather each panel at the appropriate height for the window, and crimp with vintage metal flowers, wrapping the flower stems around the fabric.

TIED-ON DETAILING (PANELS)
SKILL LEVEL
Beginner
TIME
3 hours
SUPPLIES FOR ONE
- Iron drapery rod with mounting hardware
- Shantung silk dupioni

HIGH-STYLE HARDWARE (PRINT ON RINGS)
SKILL LEVEL
Beginner
TIME
2 hours
SUPPLIES FOR ONE
- Iron hangers and rings
- Cotton print fabric
- Coordinating fabric for bows

TIED-ON DETAILING (PANELS)
(PROJECT SHOWN ON PAGE 40)

- **Measure the rod, and divide by 2**. Multiply by 2½, and add 5 inches for side hems. This measurement is for one panel width. Measure the length from the rod to the floor, adding extra to length so fabric puddles on floor. Add 4 inches for a 3½-inch hem and a ½-inch seam allowance at top. For ties subtract the distance from the rod to the top of the window (about 6 inches for these panels). Refer to the photo for guidance.
- **Determine the number of ties for each panel.** Plan for one at each end, one in the center, and evenly space remainder at 8- to 10-inch intervals.
- **From the shantung, cut two panels.** Also cut two 4-inch-wide strips the finished width of each panel plus 1 inch (for tie facings) and the determined number of 4×24-inch ties.
- **For each panel, press under ½ inch, then 2 inches at each side.** Machine-stitch. Press under ½ inch, 3 inches at the bottom edge, and hem.
- **Fold each tie in half lengthwise with right sides facing.** Stitch together, leaving an opening for turning in the middle of the long edge. Clip corners, turn right side out, and press. Fold and press each tie in half crosswise.
- **Press under ½ inch on short edges** and one long edge of each facing.
- **Pin the folded edge of each tie to the top raw edge of the panel.** Baste in place. Matching raw edges, pin and then stitch the facing to the panel (with ties in between). Press the facing to the wrong side of the panel, and hand-sew in place.
- **Tie panels to rod.**

HIGH-STYLE HARDWARE (PRINT ON RINGS)
(PROJECT SHOWN ON PAGE 52)

- **Attach hangers just below the ceiling.**
- **Measure window width, and divide by 2.** Multiply by 2½ and add 5 inches for side hems. Measure the length from the hanger hook to the floor, and add 10½ inches for hems. Cut two panels with these measurements.
- **Press under ½ inch,** then 2 inches at each side, and hand- or machine-stitch in place. Repeat for the top edge. For the hem, press under 4 inches twice, and hem.
- **Cut a 4×20-inch strip from coordinating fabric for each bow.** Make one for each hanger. Fold each strip in half lengthwise with right sides facing. Machine-stitch the long edge. Stitch one end at an angle, and trim excess fabric. Clip corners, turn right side out, and press. Tuck in raw edge at the open end, and fold to match other angle. Slip-stitch opening closed. Tie strip into a bow. Sew bows to top of curtain panels to correspond with hangers. Sew rings behind bows. Loop panels to hangers.

TIED-ON DETAILING (VALANCE AND ROMAN SHADE)

SKILL LEVEL
Beginner

TIME
1½ days

SUPPLIES FOR ONE

For the valance
- Bamboo cane and mounting hardware
- Natural solid burlap fabric
- Print fabric for the Roman shade
- All supplies under the general instructions, page 82
- Natural solid burlap fabric
- Woven-stripe burlap
- Natural eyelash fringe

TIED-ON DETAILING (VALANCE AND ROMAN SHADE)
(PROJECT SHOWN ON PAGE 41)

- **Mount the bamboo rod.** Measure the bamboo rod, and multiply by 1½. Add 1 inch for ½-inch seam allowances. This is the valance width. For the burlap valance length, measure down from the rod to the desired length, and add ½ inch for a top seam allowance. Multiply by 2. Cut one shape from the solid burlap.
- **Also from the solid burlap,** cut 2½x18-inch strips for ties. To determine number of ties, plan one at each end, one in center, and then evenly space remaining ties at 8- to 10-inch intervals.
- **Cut another valance shape from the print fabric,** making it the same width as the burlap shade, only 4 inches shorter.
- **Fold the print valance in half with right sides facing.** Sew the sides and top together, leaving an opening along the top edge for turning. Clip corners, turn right side out, and press.
- **Press under the short ends on the burlap ties,** then press them in half lengthwise. Topstitch the long edges together.
- **Fold the burlap valance in half crosswise** with right sides facing. Sew the sides. Clip corners, turn right side out, and press, turning under the top raw edge ½ inch. Hand-sew opening closed.
- **Fold each tie in half, and tack fold inside the burlap valance.** Lay the print valance over the burlap valance; then topstitch close to the top edge. Tie valance to bamboo rod.

FOR THE ROMAN SHADE. Follow the general instructions on pages 82–84 with the following exceptions/additions:

SEWING THE SHADE. After you have pressed under 4 inches at the bottom edge of the shade, cut and stitch burlap side bands as follows: Cut two 3-inch-wide bands of burlap the length of the shade minus 4 inches. Press under ½ inch on all edges of the band, and topstitch to the shade, matching the top edges.

- **Stitch across the width of the shade** 1½ inches from the bottom fold of the shade to create a rod pocket. Fold up the bottom another 4 inches. Stitch across the width near the top fold. Insert the metal rod in the pocket, then slip-stitch the pocket openings closed. Glue lengths of eyelash fringe to the wrong side of the shade at the sides and the bottom edge.

ATTACHING THE RINGS. Mark the placement of rings on the wrong side of the shade, using a water-soluble marking pen.

- **Place the first and last vertical rows about 2 inches from the sides.** Place a third vertical row in the center. Plan the top horizontal row 4 inches from the top. Plan the bottom horizontal row just above the metal rod pocket. Using thread that matches the shade fabric or clear nylon thread, hand-sew the rings in place through both the face fabric and the lining.
- **Finish the shade** as directed under the general instructions, pages 82–84.

SKILL LEVEL

Beginner

TIME

1 hour

SUPPLIES FOR ONE

- Two very long roofing nails (with round flat heads)
- Hammer
- Plaid moiré fabric
- Botanical-print polished cotton fabric
- Rubber bands

REFINED TREATMENTS (NO-SEW FLOUNCED CURTAINS)

(PROJECT SHOWN ON PAGE 43)

- **Each window treatment is made from two lengths of fabric fashioned with rubber bands.** No machine- or hand-hemming is required. If desired, you can press under narrow rolled hems on all sides, and stitch or press them in place.

- **Place a roofing nail 1 inch diagonally from one top corner of the window.** Hammer it in at an upward angle. Repeat for the other corner.

- **For the plaid length, measure from the floor to the nail,** add 12 inches for the flounced puddle on the floor, and 30 inches for the large bottom puff at the top of the window. Multiply the total by 2. Measure across the window, and add this (plus a few inches more for the swag) to the total. Divide the final measurement by 36 to determine the necessary yardage. Measure the botanical-print length as for the plaid length, except add 20 inches for the small top puff.

- **Begin at one end of the plaid length.** Gather the width into your hand. Wrap tightly with a rubber band about 1 to 2 inches from the gathered end. Place the rubber-banded area on the floor (on the left side of the window). Turn the rubber-banded area up, then wrap the raw edges of the fabric length around it.

- **Raise the fabric up to the first nail.** Holding the fabric length in your left hand, measure off 30 inches for the bottom puff. Fold this 30-inch length in half, holding it in your left hand, too. Wrap a rubber band around the two loops you have in your hand and around the nail. Don't fuss

with the shape of the puff until all fabric is in place.

- **Take the fabric over to the right side,** keeping the top edge of the fabric taut across the top of the window. Gently maneuver the bottom edge of the fabric into a soft swag; then repeat the puff technique on the right side of the window. Let the fabric fall to the floor and make another flounced puddle.

- **Repeat with the second fabric,** making smaller puffs. Adjust all puffs and swags until you are pleased with the arrangement.

- **For fabric with an obvious direction:** Cut the fabric into two lengths as follows. The first length ends when the second puff is completed. The remaining length is rubber-banded to the nail (in the correct direction) and ends in a flounced puddle.

SKILL LEVEL

Advanced

TIME

5 to 6 hours per shade

SUPPLIES FOR ONE

- See page 82.
- Red-and-white-striped cotton fabric
- Red cotton fabric
- White lining fabric

ROMANS ALWAYS WORK
(PROJECT SHOWN ON PAGES **48–49**)

- **CUTTING THE FABRICS.** Measure the inside window width and length. This is the finished size of the shade.
- **For the valance:** On tracing paper, draw a valance rectangle that measures 10 inches tall by the width of the mounting board. Add the depth of the mounting board to the top edge. Add ½ inch for seam allowances to the sides and bottom edge. Next, draw a 3½-inch-tall band pattern, making it the width of the valance pattern (including seam allowances). For the pleat pattern, draw a 6-inch-wide rectangle the height of the valance pattern (including seam allowances and header strip allowance). Cut out the patterns.
- **Cut one valance pattern from the striped fabric** (with the stripes running horizontally). Cut a border band and four pleat patterns from the red fabric. Note: The lining will be cut later.
- **For the shade:** The shade consists of three pieces—the main shade, the border, and the rod pocket. To determine the width for all three pieces, add 5 inches to the window width. Note: If you plan to hand-sew individual rings to the shade, add about ¾ inch for every 36 inches of fabric width and length to the measurements. This accommodates fabric taken up when stitching the rings in place.
- **Cut the main shade from the striped fabric** (with the stripes running vertically) to the window length plus ½ inch. Cut a 6-inch-tall band from red fabric and a 6-inch-tall rod pocket from the stripe.
- **Cut the lining fabric,** making it 3 inches narrower

and 2½ inches longer than the finished size of the shade. Note: If you need to piece the shade fabric and lining, piece them identically. It's best to plan a seam where rings (or ring tape) will be attached. See "Attaching the Rings," page 83.

SEWING THE VALANCE. Note: Sew all pieces with right sides facing and using ½-inch seam allowances. Sew the band to the bottom edge of the striped valance. Press the seam allowance toward the red fabric. Topstitch across the top of the band, if desired. Cut a lining to match.

- **Stitch a pleat to each side of the valance.** Repeat for the lining. Sew the lining to the valance, leaving open along the top edge for turning. Clip corners, turn to the right side, and press. Topstitch the opening closed. Press the pleats in half lengthwise. If desired, stitch along each pleat close to the fold. Stay-stitch across the top of the valance, securing the pleats. Set the valance aside.

SEWING THE SHADE. With right sides facing and using ½-inch seam allowances, sew the band between the striped shade and the rod pocket. Press the seams toward the (darker) red fabric.

- **Sew the lining to the pieced fabric,** and finish the top edge and rod pocket as directed in the general instructions, pages 82–84.

FINISHING THE SHADE. Follow the general instructions, pages 83–84, to attach the rings, prepare the mounting board, and thread the rings.

MOUNTING THE SHADE. Use a staple gun to secure the header strip allowance of the valance to the top of the header strip. Follow the general instructions, pages 83–84.

BATH BEAUTIES
SKILL LEVEL
Beginner
TIME
1 to 1½ days,
depending on drying
times
SUPPLIES FOR ONE
- Vinyl window shade
- Latex paint in
desired colors
- Artist's brushes
- 1 yard of 54- or
60-inch-wide cotton
duck cloth
- 1×2 wood board, 2
inches longer than the
window frame width
- Two 3-inch
L-brackets

COTTAGE GARDEN
(EASY TIE VALANCE)
SKILL LEVEL
Intermediate
TIME
2 hours
SUPPLIES FOR ONE
- 2 yards of face fabric
wider than window
- Contrasting fabric
for tie
- 1×2 wood board
- Two or three screws

BATH BEAUTIES (PAINTED WINDOW SHADE)
(PROJECT SHOWN ON PAGE 55)
- **Cut the shade to fit inside the window frame.**
Lightly sketch the design onto the shade with a
pencil. Paint the design with latex paint, allowing
each color to dry before adding another. Install
the shade.
- **Fold cotton duck cloth in half lengthwise with
wrong sides facing** so it is 18 inches tall. Cut the
fabric width 4 inches wider than the 1×2. Press
under fabric 1 inch at each end. Starting at the
center, staple the top of the fabric to the 2-inch
side of the 1×2. When the entire length of the
board is stapled, turn the board so that staples
are at the top. Wrap the ends of the fabric around
the ends of the 1×2, and staple at the back.
- **Cut two 3×36-inch strips of fabric from the
leftover fabric.** Press under the short ends; then
press the long edges to the center of the strip.
Glue in place. Paint dot designs on the strips. Let
dry before continuing with project.
- **Referring to the photo, page 55,** staple the
center of each strip at the top of the board
several inches from each side. Mount L-brackets
above the window frame. Mount the board to L-
brackets. Tie strips at the bottom to gather up the
fabric for a soft look.

COTTAGE GARDEN (EASY-TIE
STAGECOACH VALANCE)
(PROJECT SHOWN ON PAGE 59)
- **Cut the board about ¼ inch shorter than the
window width (inside mount).**
- **Measure your window width, and add 1 inch.**
The length used for the panel shown is 67
inches. **Note:** This length includes enough fabric
for a self-lining, 20 inches for the roll-up at the
bottom edge, and 1½ inches to attach it to the
board.
- **Fold the fabric in half horizontally with right
sides facing.** Stitch the edges together with a
½-inch seam allowance, leaving an opening for
turning. Clip corners, turn right side out, and
press. Slip-stitch opening closed. Staple the top
1½ inches of the valance to the top of the board.
- **Cut and piece one 5×60-inch strip of fabric for
the tie.** Fold the strip in half lengthwise with right
sides facing. Stitch raw edges together, angling
the ends and leaving an opening for turning. Trim
excess fabric, clip corners, and turn right side
out. Press; then slip-stitch the opening closed.
- **Staple the midpoint of the tie to the midpoint
on the top of the board.** Screw the board into
place. Roll up the bottom of the shade until the
center drop is 12 inches long. Tie bow to secure.

YOUNG AND FUN (POUFED PANELS)
SKILL LEVEL
Beginner
TIME
1 hour
SUPPLIES FOR ONE
- Two scarf rings with mounting hardware
- Lightweight cotton print fabric
- Tissue paper

NURSERY NAPPING
SKILL LEVEL
Advanced
TIME
4 to 5 hours per shade
SUPPLIES FOR ONE
- See page 82.
- 1×2 board, ½ inch shorter than the finished width of your shade (for the mounting board)
- Pale blue cotton fabric
- White fabric for lining and rod pocket
- White ball fringe

YOUNG AND FUN (POUFED PANELS)
(PROJECT SHOWN ON PAGE 60)
- **Determine the mounting placement for each scarf ring,** placing each one several inches above and to the outside of the door frame. Mount the rings to the wall.
- **For each panel width,** measure the width of one French door, and multiply by 1½. Add 1 inch for ½-inch seam allowances. For the length, measure from the scarf ring to the floor, adding about 12 inches for the pouf and seam allowances, and several more inches to puddle the panels on the floor. Multiply this length by 2. Cut two panels with these measurements from cotton print.
- **Fold each panel in half crosswise with right sides facing.** Sew together along the short edge and the long sides, leaving a 6-inch opening along one long side near the fold (top edge). Clip corners, turn right side out, and press.
- **Pull the top edge of each panel through a ring,** stuffing tissue paper into the opening. Hand-sew the opening closed.

NURSERY NAPPING
(PROJECT SHOWN ON PAGES 50–51)
PREPARING THE MOUNTING BOARD. Measure the window width, starting and ending in the center of the side molding. This is the finished width of the shade.
- **Paint the mounting board or cover it with fabric;** then temporarily secure it to the window molding. You can screw it directly to the molding or secure it with two L-brackets (see the diagrams, page 83).

CUTTING THE FABRICS. You already have established the finished width. For the length, measure from the top of the header strip to the sill. This is the finished size of the shade.
- **Add 5 inches to the width measurement** and 2½ inches to the length. Note: If you plan to hand-sew individual rings to the shade, add about ¾ inch to these measurements for every 36 inches of fabric width and length. This accommodates fabric taken up when stitching the rings in place. Cut a rectangle with these measurements from the pale blue fabric.
- **Cut the lining fabric,** making it 3 inches narrower than the finished size of the shade and 2½ inches longer. Note: If you need to piece the shade fabric and lining for the project, piece them identically. It's best to plan a seam where rings (or ring tape) will be attached. See "Attaching the Rings," page 83.
- **For the rod pocket,** cut a 2½-inch-wide strip the width of the finished shade plus 1 inch from lining fabric. Press under ½ inch on all edges. Set aside.

SEWING THE SHADE. Place the two fabrics together with right sides facing; align the top edges and one side. Stitch along the side using a ½-inch seam allowance. Now align the opposite sides (the face fabric is wider than the lining). Stitch this seam. Press both seams open. Turn the shade right side out. Center the lining on the back of the shade, and press again.

■ **At the top edge, press under ½ inch,** then 2 inches. Stitch in place.

■ **Make a pattern for the scalloped edge.** Draw a line on tracing paper the finished width of the shade. Divide the line into thirds; then make a scallop in one of the sections. Use a plate or a compass to create the curve. Trace the curve two more times. Cut out the pattern, and place it along the bottom edge of the shade. Draw scallops on the front of the shade using a water-soluble marking pen. Stay-stitch ¼ inch inside the scallops. Cut out scalloped edge on marking pen lines. Glue or topstitch white ball fringe in place.

■ **Pin the rod pocket on the wrong side** of the shade just above the scalloped edge. Stitch the long edges only, sewing through both layers. Insert the metal rod in the pocket, then slip-stitch the pocket openings closed.

ATTACHING THE RINGS. See the general instructions, page 83.

PREPARING THE MOUNTING BOARD. Remove the header strip from the window frame. Press one side of the hook-and-loop fastening tape across the front (long narrow) edge of the mounting board, and the other side of the tape to the wrong side of the shade across the top edge. To mount the shade to the mounting board, press the hook-and-loop fastening tape together.

■ **Next, mark points on the underside of the mounting board** for the placement of screw eyes. The screw eyes must correspond with the vertical row of rings. Attach the screw eyes at each point.

THREADING THE RINGS. See the general instructions, page 83.

MOUNTING THE SHADE. Secure the mounting board to the window frame, then finish as directed in the general instructions, page 83.

■ **Mount the awning cleat to the right of the window.** Pull on the cording lengths to make sure the shade pulls up evenly, then release the shade. Braid the cording lengths together and knot at the end. Wrap the braided length around the awning cleat to hold the Roman shade at the desired level.

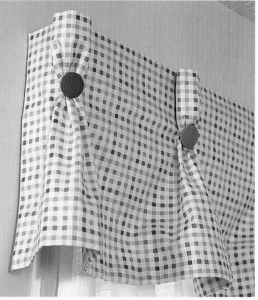

COTTAGE GARDEN (BUTTONED VALANCE OVER SHEERS)

SKILL LEVEL

Beginner

TIME

4 hours

SUPPLIES FOR ONE

- One 1×4 board, at least 2 inches longer than the window width, including the frame
- Batting to cover mounting board
- 1¼ yards of lining fabric
- ⅝ yard of 54-inch-wide face fabric
- Two L-brackets with screws (to mount the mounting board to the window)
- Four 1⅞-inch-diameter self-covering buttons
- Fabric scraps for buttons (pink, green, and purple)
- Ready-made sheers
- Spring-tension rod

COTTAGE GARDEN (BUTTONED VALANCE OVER SHEERS)

(PROJECT SHOWN ON PAGE **58**)

- **Cover the mounting board with batting and lining fabric.**
- **Plan the number of pleats first,** placing one at each corner of the mounting board, one in the center, then evenly spacing additional pleats at 8- to 10-inch intervals.
- **To determine the valance width,** add the returns (8 inches) to the long measurement of the mounting board. Add 1 inch for each pleat and 1 inch for ½-inch seam allowances.
- **For the valance length,** add 1 inch for ½-inch seam allowances to the determined finished length (this valance is 18 inches long).
- **Cut one rectangle with these measurements from face fabric.** Cut the lining the same width as the face fabric, but 2 inches shorter.
- **With right sides facing,** sew the lining and face fabric together along the top edge. Now align the bottom edges (the lining is shorter, so the face fabric will "buckle"). Stitch the bottom edge. Press this seam open. Do not turn right side out. Press the valance from the lining side, starting at the top and working to the bottom (2 inches of the fabric will be ironed to the wrong side of the valance).
- **Stitch the sides,** leaving an opening for turning. Clip corners, turn right side out, and press. Slip-stitch opening closed.
- **Mark a small dot 4 inches from each end** at the top edge of the valance. Evenly divide the remainder of the fabric for 1-inch pleats and

equal spaces.

- **Gather and pin pleats,** then hand-tack in place.
- **Cover buttons with fabric scraps.** Sew a covered button to each gathered pleat.
- **Pin the 4-inch returns to each side of the mounting board,** placing the top of the valance 3 to 4 inches above the board. Hand-sew the valance to the board. Mount the covered 1×4 above the window with L-brackets (see diagram, page 84).
- **Add sheers mounted on a spring-tension rod.**

MAPS OF THE WORLD (VALANCE)

SKILL LEVEL

Beginner

TIME

30 minutes

SUPPLIES FOR ONE

- Brass hanging rod and mounting hardware
- World map
- Flat jute trim and jute cord
- Sage green roller shade
- Brass curtain clips
- Toy compass (for shade pull)
- Plastic-paper adhesive

MAPS OF THE WORLD (SHADE)

SKILL LEVEL

Beginner

TIME

30 minutes

SUPPLIES FOR ONE

- Vinyl roller shade kit (same kit used for fabric-covered shades)
- World map
- Pressing cloth

MAPS OF THE WORLD (VALANCE)

(PROJECT SHOWN ON PAGE 65)

- **Mount the hanging rod.**
- **Draw a valance rectangle on tracing paper to the desired width and length.** Add 2 inches to the length. Cut out. Check rectangle size against the window, and adjust if necessary.
- **Place the rectangle over the center of the map, and lightly trace around it.** Cut out the map rectangle, trimming around land masses and lettering along the bottom edge. Fold under the top 2 inches of the valance. Set aside.
- **Referring to the photo,** page 65, glue jute trim across the bottom of the sage green shade. Remove the ring from one brass curtain clip, and add the compass. Clip to the shade for a pull. Cut motifs from the leftover map paper, and glue to the shade. Mount shade, then clip valance in place. Drape a length of jute cord across the hanging rod.

MAPS OF THE WORLD (SHADE)

(PROJECT SHOWN ON PAGE 64)

- **Trim the roller shade to fit the window.** Lay the map right side down and place the shade on top. Trace around the shade. Cut out the map, and iron it to the treated side of the vinyl roller shade, using a press cloth to protect the paper. Install the shade.

YOUNG AND FUN (PENNANT-STYLE VALANCES)

SKILL LEVEL

Beginner

TIME

1 hour per window

SUPPLIES FOR ONE

For single-point valance
- 1×2 wood strip, ¼ to ½ inch shorter than the width of your window (for the mounting board)

For multiple-point valance
- 1×4 wood strip, the width of the window from frame to frame (mounting board for an outside mount)
- Wall paint for both
- Two-color block fabric
- Lining fabric
- Black fabric
- Adhesive hook-and-loop fastening tape
- L-brackets and screws

YOUNG AND FUN (PENNANT-STYLE VALANCES)
(PROJECT SHOWN ON PAGE 61)

SINGLE-POINT VALANCE. Mount the wood strip to the window (see diagram, page 83).

- **On tracing paper,** draw a rectangle the width of the mounting board and the desired length of the color block fabric. Cut out the rectangle. Fold rectangle in half lengthwise and open. Draw diagonal lines from the bottom of the fold to the top corners. Add a 2-inch border to the triangle, taping extra paper at the bottom to accommodate the point. Cut out the pattern, and check against the window.

- **Draw around the pattern on the color block fabric.** Draw a ½-inch seam allowance all around. Do not cut out.

- **Cut 4-inch strip(s) across the width of black fabric.** Press the long raw edges to the center. Pin the band to the seam line on one side of the triangle. Trim excess even with the side seam allowances. Topstitch in place. Repeat for the other side, except turn under the short edge at the point to mimic a mitered corner. Topstitch in place. Cut out the banded triangle and a matching lining.

- **With right sides facing,** and ½-inch seams, sew the lining to the face fabric, leaving an opening for turning. Clip corners, turn right side out, and press. Sew the opening closed.

- **Attach one half of the hook-and-loop fastening tape across the top of the valance.** Attach the other half to the front of the mounting board. Mount valance to board.

MULTIPLE-POINT VALANCE. Paint the

wood strip with the wall color, then mount with L-brackets above the window (see diagram, page 84).

- **On tracing paper,** draw a rectangle the width of the mounting board and the desired length of the color block fabric. Add the returns to each side. Cut out the rectangle. Fold rectangle in half lengthwise and open. Draw a V in the center and one (or more) on each side, stopping at the returns. Add a 2-inch border as for the single-point treatment. Cut out the pattern, and check against the window.

- **Stitch and mount this valance as directed for the single-point window.**

ART OF THE SHADE (BANDED ROMAN SHADE)

SKILL LEVEL

Advanced

TIME

5 hours

SUPPLIES FOR ONE

- Supplies for Roman shade, page 82.
- Rooster print fabric
- Tone-on-tone yellow-striped fabric
- White or ivory lining fabric

ART OF THE SHADE (BANDED ROMAN SHADE)
(PROJECT SHOWN ON PAGES 66–67,70–71)

CUTTING THE FABRICS. Measure the inside window width and length. This is the finished size of the shade.

- **Subtract 4 inches from the finished width** and 4 inches from the finished length. **Note:** If you plan to hand-sew individual rings to the shade, add about ¾ inch to the measurements for every 36 inches of fabric width and length. This accommodates fabric taken up when stitching the rings in place.

- **Cut a rectangle with these measurements from the rooster print.** Using a light pencil or chalk, mark the right side of the rectangle with a ½-inch seam allowance.

- **For the top and bottom bands,** cut two 3½-inch-wide strips from the yellow-striped fabric, making them as long as the finished shade width plus 7 inches. For the side bands, cut two 3½-inch-wide strips as long as the finished shade length plus 7 inches.

SEWING THE SHADE. With right sides facing, center and pin the bands to the rooster print. Stitch in place, starting and stopping at the marked seam allowance. Fold two adjacent borders together with the right sides facing. Mark a 45-degree diagonal line from the corner seam line to the corner of the border. Stitch, then trim the excess fabric. Repeat for each corner.

- **Measure the depth of the mounting board,** and add 1 inch (for ½-inch seam allowances). From yellow-striped fabric, cut a band to this measurement, long enough to fit across the top

of the bordered fabric. From yellow striped fabric, cut an 8½-inch band to fit across the bottom of the bordered fabric. Using ½-inch seam allowances, sew these bands to the top and bottom of the bordered fabric. Cut a matching shape from the lining, only cut the lining length 8 inches shorter.

- **With right sides facing and the top edge even,** sew the lining to the bordered fabric along the sides and top. Clip corners, turn to the right side, and press.

- **Press under 4 inches at the bottom of the shade.** Stitch across the width of the shade 1½ inches from the fold to create a rod pocket. Fold up the bottom another 4 inches. Stitch across the width near the top fold. Insert the metal rod in the pocket, then slip-stitch the pocket openings closed.

ATTACHING THE RINGS. See the general instructions, page 83.

PREPARING THE MOUNTING BOARD. Paint the mounting board to match your window frame, or cover it with lining fabric.

- **Using a staple gun,** staple the top band of the shade to the top of the mounting board.

- **Next, mark points on the underside of the header strip for the placement of screw eyes.** The screw eyes must correspond with the vertical row of rings on the shade. Screw the screw eyes to each point.

THREADING THE RINGS. See the general instructions, page 83.

MOUNTING THE SHADE. See the general instructions, pages 83–84.

WINDOW-SIDE DINING
SKILL LEVEL
Advanced
TIME
2 to 3 days, including drying time
SUPPLIES FOR ONE
- ½-inch plywood as follows:
- One 48×20-inch piece for front section (adjust width)
- Two 4½×20-inch pieces for returns
- One 4½×48-inch piece
- Decorative molding
- Band saw
- Small finishing nails
- Miter box
- White enamel paint
- 1-inch flat paintbrush
- Blue interior paint
- No. 8 round artist's brush
- L-brackets and screws
- Ready-made ivory linen panels
- Accent fabric
- Fusible interfacing

WINDOW-SIDE DINING (APPLIQUE BORDER AND CORNICE)
(PROJECT SHOWN ON PAGE 75)
- **Draw a scallop on top of the front section.** Cut the scalloped edge with a band saw. Attach return pieces to both ends of the front section with wood glue and small finishing nails.
- **Attach the interior support from the back,** lowering it 4½ inches from the top so it won't be seen above the cutout scallop. Attach it perpendicularly to the front section (with the ½-inch side glued down to make a shelf). Attach with wood glue and finishing nails. This stabilizes the unit and provides a means of attachment to the wall. Add decorative molding to the bottom edge, mitering the corners. Glue into place and nail.
- **Prime the cornice.** When dry, paint with white enamel paint. Let dry.
- **With a 1-inch flat paintbrush dipped in blue paint,** paint vertical lines across the cornice, spacing them 5 inches apart. Note: For best results, work out the spacing pattern on paper before painting the cornice. Use the artist's brush to paint stripes on each side of the vertical line (see photograph).
- **After the vertical lines are dry,** repeat with horizontal lines. Handpaint a border around the edges with the 1-inch paintbrush.
- **Set the cornice over the window, and mount from the top side with L-brackets.**
- **Decorate ready-made linen tie-top draperies with scalloped appliquéd borders.** For the border, cut two 5½-inch-wide strips of accent fabric the

length of the panel plus 1 inch for ½-inch seam allowances.
- **Trace the scallop repeat for the cornice on white paper for a pattern and cut out.** Trace and repeat the pattern along the length of the accent fabric strips, making a left and a right. Cut out.
- **Cut two 5-inch-wide strips of fusible interfacing.** Trace and repeat the same scallop pattern along one edge of each strip, and cut out.
- **Place the fusible interfacing on top of the ready-made curtain panels,** matching the straight edges. Pin the accent strips on top of the interfacing, matching the scalloped edges. Fuse these pieces to the panels following the manufacturer's instructions. Pin the excess ½ inch on the accent strip to the wrong side of each curtain panel. Do the same at the top and bottom of the strips.
- **Using a straight stitch,** topstitch along the top, bottom, and straight inside edges of the panel. With a zigzag or appliqué stitch, sew the scalloped side in place.

OFFICE EASY (VINTAGE FRENCH FEED SACKS)

SKILL LEVEL

Beginner

TIME

30 minutes to 1 hour

SUPPLIES FOR ONE

- Six ½-inch-diameter brass (or plastic) rings
- Vintage French feed sack or appropriate substitute
- Clear nylon thread
- Nylon cording
- 1×2 wood strip, cut the width of the feed sack opening (for the mounting board)
- Two L-brackets with screws (to mount the mounting board to the window)
- Low-temperature glue gun

OFFICE EASY (VINTAGE FRENCH FEED SACKS)
(PROJECT SHOWN ON PAGE 77)

- **Mark placement for three rings on the back of the feed sack on one long side.** Mark one dot at the bottom corner, another in the center, and the third in between. Mark the opposite side in the same manner. Using clear nylon thread, hand-sew a brass ring to each dot.
- **Cut two pieces of cording the length of the feed sack.** Tie the end of one piece of cording to the bottom ring. Thread the cording through the remaining two rings. Repeat for the other side.
- **Slip the open end of the feed sack onto the board, and glue in place.** Mount the board above the door with L-brackets (see the general instructions for Roman shades on page 82).
- **Pull the nylon cording to create the desired folds in the feed sack.** Secure the cording to the board with glue (or hand-sew in place).

index

CONTRIBUTORS/RESOURCES

Pages 8-15: Ana Christopher and Dolores DeVries; project design; Andrea Caughey, regional editor; Ed Gohlich, photography
Pages 16-17, 19-21: Elaine Miller, project design
Page 18: Hal Davis, project design
Pages 16-27; 30-31, 62: Wade Scherrer, styling; Scott Little, photography
Pages 22-27, 30-31: Wade Scherrer, project design
Pages 28-29, 34-35, 38-39, 52-53, 56-57, 76-77: Judy Elkhouri, design and fabrication;

Nancy Ingram, regional editor; Jenifer Jordan, photography
Pages 32-33, 58-59, 75: Tina Blanck, paint project design; Susan Andrews, regional editor; Bob Greenspan, photography; Melissa Chabino, treatment fabrication
Pages 36, 48-49, 66-67, 70-71, 73 (left): Donna Talley Wendt, regional contributor; Tria Giovan, photography
Pages 37, 55, 63: Brian Carter, project design and styling; Emily Minton-Redfield, photography
Pages 40-42; 43 (lower right), 60-61: J. Edwards Interiors, Birmingham, AL; Shannon Jernigan, regional contributor; Randy Foulds, photography
Page 43 (upper right): Jean Lange Interior Design; Sally Mauer, regional editoir; Bob Mauer, photography
Pages 44: Jeff Jones, design; Pieter Estersohn, photography
Page 45: Jamie Drake, design; Pieter Estersohn, photography
Pages 46-47, 64-65: Sarah C. Duquette, design; Sam Gray, photography
Pages 50-51: Sally Dixon, project design; Andrea Caughey, regional editor; Ed Gohlich, photography
Pages 56-57: Wendy Owen, design; Heather Lobdell, regional contributor; Jamie Hadley, photography
Page 74: Paula Rice, design; Pieter Estersohn, photography
Page 75: Craig Chabino, woodworking

MATERIALS/FABRICATION

Pages 22-23 (bay window): Fabric courtesy of Meyer Drapery Services Inc., Champaign, IL, 217/352-5318; fax 217/352-5615
Pages 22-23 (bay window), 31: Hardware courtesy of Lundy's Ornamental Iron, 800/468-6040; fax 978/468-1280
Pages 32-33: Pull-up drapery panel courtesy of Umbra, 800/387-5122
Page 36: Drapery panels courtesy of Country Curtains, 800/456-0321
Page 36, 48-49, 70-71: Sewing work room, Val Paper, The Shade Place
Pages 36, 48-49, 58-59, 70-71, 75: Fabric Courtesy of Calico Corners, 800/213-6366
Page 41: Fabric and trim, King Cotton, Birmingham, AL; bamboo rod, At Home Furnishings, Birmingham, AL

U.S. UNITS TO METRIC EQUIVALENTS

To Convert From	Multiply By	To Get
Inches	25.4	Millimeters (mm)
Inches	2.54	Centimeters (cm)
Feet	30.48	Centimeters (cm)
Feet	0.3048	Meters (m)

METRIC UNITS TO U.S. EQUIVALENTS

To Convert From	Multiply By	To Get
Millimeters	0.0394	Inches
Centimeters	0.3937	Inches
Centimeters	0.0328	Feet
Meters	3.2808	Feet

M7073-B   94